Australian Place Name Stories

Australian Place Name Stories

Ruth Wajnryb

Lothian
BOOKS

Lothian Books
An imprint of Time Warner Book Group Australia
132 Albert Road, South Melbourne, 3205
www.lothian.com.au

National Library of Australia
Cataloguing-in-Publication data:

Wajnryb, Ruth, 1948– .
Australian place name stories

ISBN 0 7344 0623 1.

1. Names, Geographical - Australia. 2. Australia - Name.
3. Australia - Historical geography. I. Title.

919.4003

Cover design by Kate van de Stadt
Text design by Mary Egan
Typeset by Egan-Reid, Auckland, New Zealand
Printed in Australia by Griffin Press

Part of knowing is the act of naming.

JM Arthur, The Default Country: A Lexical Cartography of Twentieth-century Australia, 2003

Rains fell, season after season, and the sun slid up over the ridges as it had done since the beginning. The river filled and shrank with tides and floods, trees grew and died and melted back into the dirt that had given them life. Ten years made no impression on the shape of the river, of the convoluted ridges that hid it. Only down on the flats was there change, and that was mostly a matter of names.

Kate Grenville, The Secret River, 2005

On the pristine hills he built malls. Near a hallowed battle-ground, he built a subdivision. Ironically he named his cookie-cutter projects after the landscape he was destroying — Rolling Meadows, Whispering Oaks, Forest Hill.

John Grisham, The King of Torts, 2003

Contents

Acknowledgements

I wish to thank Averill Chase of Lothian Books for the idea of this book and for her help and counsel throughout the project. Averill is a unique blend of passion and efficiency, and a gem of support for a writer. The team that works with her follows her example.

I've been fortunate indeed to have had the services of two dedicated research assistants — Rachel Kenyon and Mark Cherry. I thank them for their contribution to the work.

Special thanks go to many people who shared with me their knowledge of and enthusiasm for Australian place names. Foremost here are David Blair, Flavia Hodges, Susan Poetsch, and the team at Macquarie University (NSW), including contributors to *Placenames Australia*, the newsletter of the Australian National Placenames Survey, which started out in March 1996 as the *Bulletin*, edited by Bill Noble.

I am grateful for the contribution of place name boards across the states and territories of Australia; to previously published works about place names (see References, p. 227); as well as precious labour-of-love local histories that are too numerous to list by name.

Other contributions came from Lorraine Bayliss, Dawn Cohen, Julie Dowling, W J (Bill) Forrest, Brian Goodchild, Tina Graham, Jan Ireland, Tony Naughton, the late Christopher Richards, and Greg Windsor.

Errors of course remain my responsibility, and where they have occurred, by omission or commission, I would be pleased to be advised, for subsequent reprints. Furthermore, if a reader wants to share a place name story of interest, I would be pleased to consider it for the next edition. Please contact the publishers.

Ruth Wajnryb
Sydney, 2006

Introduction

Names bespeak history and so are rarely value-free. In *Living Black: Blacks Talk to Kevin Gilbert*, Kevin Gilbert writes, 'Ask white or black Australian kids to name a heroic Red Indian chief or a famous Indian tribe and most will be able to do so because of comics and films. Ask them to name an Aboriginal hero or a famous Aboriginal tribe and they will not be able to do so because Aboriginal history is either unknown or negative.' A quarter of a century after that was written, not much has changed.

Names matter. Shakespeare was wrong to have Juliet say what she did about roses. They actually smell as good as they do in part by virtue of their name. The nose familiar with the fragrance of rose will invest the word with its knowledge so that the very expectation of rose will be invested in the word. That's why 'rose' smells differently from, say, 'frog'.

Now that's not to suggest that in the coinage any one-to-one correspondence exists between a word (for example, 'dog') and the thing the word represents (woof-emitting, tail-wagging, four-legged creature). But words over time come to mean their names. Names gather moss the way rolling stones do not.

Take place names. Key 'Macquarie' into Google and you get 470000 hits. Unsurprisingly, the colonial powerbrokers who did the naming had a habit of honouring themselves. But one person's honour is another's ignominy. Names have connotations that are emotional, context-dependent and subjective. For more than two hundred years, indigenous people have put up with colonial names dominating what was once their landscape.

Do we ever think what that must be like? Yes we do — during World War I, most of the German place names in South Australia were changed, in acknowledgement of the national enemy (then many were changed back in the 1930s, fuelled by the prospect of commercial links with then Nazi Germany). So we know the feeling, but we rarely extrapolate.

Of course, history is written by the victors. Waterloo would not have its English significance had the victor's shoe been on Napoleon's foot. And many local place names have indigenous connections, though they're mostly roughshod and unverifiable. Tasmania, interestingly, has almost no place names honouring the Aboriginal connection. Hands up who knows why that might be.

I used to know a tour guide in Israel where guiding is highly prestigious, if lowly paid. There you need to know a few languages, have a deep knowledge of history, archaeology and theology, among other disciplines, and a fine appreciation of how these intersect with topography and toponymy. My friend was from South Africa, and her Afrikaans allowed her to communicate with Dutch tour groups. These were mostly organised, church-based groups, who found it discombobulating that the scripture-book Holy Land toponymy in their heads didn't match the Hebrew place names they encountered; nor did the names they used for the principal characters in the Nativity story match those they heard being used about them. Names are important. Scratch at the topsoil a bit and you'll find memory below.

I've come to think of place names as moments in history that are freeze-framed for posterity. As such, the values embedded in the name remain frozen and may later jar with changing social values. A good example is found in a recent controversy over place names in the United States containing the word 'squaw', for example, Squaw Peak, of which there are seventy-three in Arizona alone. Popular belief, undeterred by lack of evidence, has it that 'squaw' is a Mohawk word for female genitalia. Yet American Indians' petitions for 'squaw' to be replaced in official place names have mostly fallen on deaf white ears — the request being dismissed as 'silly'.

But of course it isn't silly. It's time we acknowledged the values we assert and those we deny through our place-naming conventions. As Bruce Pascoe (2003) puts it, 'It's about recognising how today's Australians came by their country . . . respecting the history . . . and honouring those who named this great land and still live here.'

A new look at place names

> Placenames are not just facts about the world or word-objects that we manipulate. They have a life of their own, and they have a living place in our culture. They are part of our cultural and social history. They act as cultural signposts revealing much about our cultural history, if we care to look ... Researching [them] is the process of writing their 'biographies'. Each name ... was given by somebody to a particular place, at a particular time, for a particular reason.
>
> Blair 2004

As a culture, white Australians generally live very much in the now. If we face any direction at all, it's forward, looking toward the future. Perhaps because white settlement is only a few hundred years old, many of us have precious little knowledge of the past; and we lack interest in what we don't know. Significantly, we're ignorant of how much we don't know.

Perhaps we haven't had the span of time to dig deeply into the soil and feel a true 'belongingness' with place. This may be why so few among us truly appreciate the indigenous people's attachment to the land or the spiritual significance of 'place'. Personally, I had to travel abroad, and recognise attachment to soil — in places as far-flung as South Africa and Israel — before returning home to Australia to realise that a similar connection exists here, if you look for it.

Not surprisingly, really, those of us who are heirs to European settlement in Australia have a utilitarian approach to place names. We normally pay little attention to a place name other than consider it an address for snail mail or note it on the map if we're driving through. Life is so rushed and people are so time-poor that we rarely stop to wonder where a name came from, what its origin was, what people who lived before us once thought or intended. We don't treat a name as an artefact, the way an archaeologist or anthropologist might. We don't consider that there's a story there, lying beneath, awaiting a probe and a question.

Prior to European settlement, the indigenous peoples around the continent had named the landscape of their world. When the explorers came in their ships, they gave names to things they encountered on their travels. There were waves of such explorers — the Portuguese, the Dutch, the French, and the English — and their footprints can be seen in the places around the coast that they named.

Australian toponymy distinguishes between indigenous and introduced place names, and within the latter category it distinguishes between pre- and post-1788. Prior to 1788, introduced names are mostly a function of exploratory navigation of the coastlines. After settlement began in 1788, in the early days of the colony, the naming of settlements and towns, as well as topographical features such as hills, mountains, rivers and lakes, was quite a casual business. It was a way of remembering or honouring friends, benefactors and dignitaries. It may have softened the longing for home. Very often the names imperfectly adopted local Aboriginal words that were thought to be used as place names. Sometimes names commemorated an incident; sometimes they reflected social position or served the purpose of self-aggrandisement.

This book takes a fresh look at place names using history and narrative as the guiding tools. Here the starting point is to consider a place name as the label people in the past have attached with deliberation to a geographical area. The people themselves have mostly long gone, but the name remains and under it, as it were, may be found stories that momentarily revive the past and make it available to us today. And there is no shortage to choose from. At the end of the twentieth century, there were more than four million Australian place names of which approximately three-quarters have Aboriginal origins (Kennedy 1989).

It's these little narratives that make up the substance of the book. The material is organised alphabetically, and includes place names from every state and territory. Interspersed among the entries are 'themed' boxes containing additional information of interest relating to place names of Australia.

Truth, myth and history

It is a fair enough question to ask whether the stories behind the names in this book are 'true' or whether and how they have been authenticated. Truth is not an easy matter to pin down, in toponymy, history or the law court. And the processes of authentication are equally difficult. In many cases, sources and records are long gone, and a story has evolved that may have moved some distance from the original sound, as in the children's game of Chinese whispers (Kostanski 2003).

I am less worried about this than may at first glance seem proper. Reflecting on it, I have come to understand better the relationship between truth, myth and history. It's a connection described elegantly in a book about Australian place names (Whittaker & Willesee 2002). In it the point is made, originally by writer Peter Carey in a letter to a Tom Baxter of Derby, Western Australia, and told by Baxter to the authors. Carey and Baxter were communicating on the subject of Ned Kelly, Carey having written a book on him, and Baxter having possession of Kelly's skull. Carey apparently introduced Baxter 'to the idea that [Ned Kelly] occupies the place in Australia that George Washington and Abraham Lincoln occupy in the US.' He said, *'The truth is in the myth, not in the history'* (2002, p. 109, italics added).

I like this, not only because it removes from my shoulders the historian's obligation to authenticate, corroborate and check for reliability, but also because it affirms and legitimises the power of oral traditions, and the notion of history as the way ordinary people lived their lives and believed their beliefs. They're often not the ones who appear in the history books or on the front of monuments. It's a kind of history from below, which, as it happens, suits my own interests and ideology.

Place naming in the past

Place naming in the early days of white settlement in Australia was much more ad hoc and unregulated than it is today. As navigators navigated and explorers explored and settlers settled, places were named as the need emerged. Certainly the process then was far less bureaucratic than it is today. Even so, place naming in the colonial days was nonetheless not totally random. An analysis reveals that underlying the allocation of names was a set of conventions and assumptions that seem implicitly to have guided people's decision-making (Flavia Hodges, personal correspondence, 2005). Nine discrete categories were used.

1. Descriptive

Descriptive names drew on immediate features of the topography, such as Bare Island, Mount Abrupt, Acacia Creek and Mount Lofty. Sometimes, the naming happened by association; for example, Mount Buffalo (Vic) was named by Hume and Hovell because of its apparent resemblance to the head of a buffalo; and the nearby Buffalo River and Lake Buffalo were named by association. The West Australian township of Latham was named after Latham Rock, a large granite rock about 3 kilometres south-east of the townsite, the name Latham honouring an early pastoralist of the region.

Amply represented in the descriptive category are names drawn from local flora and fauna. Dead Gum Lake and Wattle Flat are what-you-see-is-what-you-get names, as are the many names derived from the animal kingdom, with all manner of reptiles, kangaroos, koalas, sheep, bullocks, cows, horses, dogs, cats, birds, sharks and whales, among others. (See Horses, p. 98.)

2. Personal names

This category includes first names and surnames (for example, Adelaide, Sydney, Hobart and Macquarie), sometimes in the form of conventional compounds (Blanchetown, Mortdale and Erskineville). Sometimes, it would seem the commemoration was one step removed — for example, Campbelltown (NSW) honours the maiden name of Governor Macquarie's wife. Some of these names have a commemorative function, honouring not only public figures (for example, Parkes in NSW after Sir Henry Parkes, the father of Australian Federation) but also ordinary people. These are sometimes called 'tribute names'. On occasion, the person honoured was living around the time of the naming, for example, a young horseman who gave his name to Frew River (NT). Other times, a person is being honoured in death, for example, an early copper miner and pioneer (Noltenius Billabong, NT). The use of proper names was not limited to people: Coolangatta (QLD) was named after a ship that was wrecked there; Yarrana Heights (WA) was named after a helicopter that was used in mapping the area in 1957.

Often, the naming has a possessive connotation more than a commemorative one, for instance, the NSW town of Brodies Plains. Sometimes it is a deliberate statement of affection — the town of Norseman (WA) was named after a gold prospector's horse. Sometimes, it is a committee decision, for instance, when it comes to naming electoral districts, shires and even capital cities, such as Canberra and all its suburbs and streets. (See National Celebrities, p. 34.)

3.   Names from back home

As was the custom in the opening up of the New World (think of New York, New Jersey), many names originated in the countries of origin of the settlers, for example, Newcastle, Ipswich, Perth, Dundee, Llanelly, Killarney, Bexley, Hopetoun, Leinster, Londonberry, Northampton, Rothesay and Sorrento. Another term for this is 'transplanted names'. Sometimes a perceived topographical resemblance guided the naming, for example, New South Wales, but often it would seem that nostalgia alone did. Like the early English painters of the Australian landscape, whose memories of home affected what they thought they saw and consequently painted, so too, I suspect, was the naming of places in the local landscape that reminded people of home in a highly subjective process.

4.   Incidents

Many colourful names find their source in an actual incident that occurred at or near the site — such as Blunder Creek (QLD) and Ophthalmia Range (WA). The precariousness of the early explorations and the hazards of early settlement life are often memorialised in place names. (See Pessimistic names, p. 165.)

5.   Coinage

Some names were formulated words, coined for their specific associations. Australind (WA) was named in 1841 by the West Australian Land Company, which hoped to develop trade between Australia and India. The Sydney suburb of Lidcombe was named in 1914 in honour of the mayor (Lidbury) and the former mayor (Larbombe).

6. Commendations

Some names are linked to the topography with an element of positive associations, which makes them often sound like real estate coinages, for example, Fairview, a pastoral station in Queensland; Seaforth, a northern waterside suburb of Sydney.

7. Popular etymology

This category is for names that have been reshaped by popular usage. An example is Coal and Candle Creek, located in the Kuring-gai Chase National Park (NSW). It is said to derive from an Aboriginal form transcribed as Kolaan Kandahl, though no plausible meaning for this has been suggested.

8. Mistakes

Sometimes names change through a garbled transmission process. An example is Dee Why, a northern suburb of Sydney, which was recorded in surveyor James Meehan's journal as Dy Beach; and Tylers Pass, named after swimmer David Theile, a name that a surveyor heard (if indistinctly) on his short-wave radio after the announcement of the 1960 Australian swimming champions. Mount Kokeby (WA) is a misspelling of the original Rokeby (after the Baron Rokeby of Armagh). (See Mistakes and apocrypha, p. 139.)

9. Indigenous words

The Aboriginal heritage contained in place names is massive. It's calculated that in some districts more than 90 per cent of all place names derive from Aboriginal words and around the country, it's rarely less than 40 per cent (Pascoe 2003). Some examples are Wagga Wagga, Toowoomba, Maroubra and Maroochydore. However, it is not always immediately apparent which names are indigenous in origin. For example, 'Ulladulla . . . is most probably *not*, whereas Tin Can Bay almost certainly is' (Appleton 1992).

Given the place of the land as the sacred centrepiece in Aboriginal culture and religion, it is no wonder that place naming owes so much to the indigenous languages. In fact, the features of the landscape 'are seen as icons within a vast cathedral continually occupied by Aboriginal people whose fundamental existence is the bond between the land, people and spirituality' <http://www.icsm.gov.au/icsm/cgna/aboriginal_names.pdf>.

However, the names that today we associate with Aborigines are usually white settlers' versions of Aboriginal words. They may have been misheard originally or even if heard correctly, distorted in the mouths of those unfamiliar with the sound systems of the languages about them. Sometimes the name is maintained but it is used to refer to something different from its original designation. Misinformation and ignorance played significant roles in the decision to adopt many names thought to be indigenous. Sometimes the words were randomly plucked from word lists. Later, developers subdividing land and looking for names to call the new parcels, selected Aboriginal names from books. The word 'Bellbowrie', for instance, was thought to mean a red-flowering tree; it did not reflect the local indigenous origins, but served as a pretty name for a new area opening up in Queensland in the early 1970s. Because of the difficulties of verification, given the loss of many languages and dialects (two-thirds are dead or fading), and the peoples who speak them, many names have ended up more as folk etymology.

Place naming today

Place naming today is far from a random process. All Australian states and territories are now members of the Committee for Geographical Names of Australasia (CGNA), which has agreed to a national standardised approach to place naming. Its mission is: 'as the national focus group, to coordinate and communicate the consistent use of geographic place names, to meet community requirements'. The CGSM (the Committee for Geographical Surveying and Mapping) is part of a larger body, the Intergovernmental Committee for Surveying and Mapping (ICSM).

The process of place name proposal varies a little with the particular jurisdiction. Broadly, one makes a proposal with the support of one's local government body to a state or territory Geographical Names Board. This body consults with the community and then recommends to a Minister who gazettes the name. This means the name is formalised through the legislative process. Most states and territories have documents on their websites that tell people how to go about proposing a place name or a change to an existing place name.

The criteria by which a place name is accepted or rejected reflect a range of concerns — for instance, an interest in consistency, a concern to reflect history and indigenous origins, and care to avoid offence, ambiguity or confusion. The list below has been adapted from the website of the NSW Geographical Names Board and is typical of the concerns that are involved in place naming.

- A name suggested for any place that owes its origin to the peculiarity of the topographical feature designated, such as shape, vegetation and animal life, may be accepted but, in doing so, care should be exercised in avoiding duplication of names already used for other features. The preference is to avoid the repetition of commonly used names (for example, Sugar Loaf, Sandy Bank, Bald Mountain and Reedy Spring).

- Easily pronounced names are preferred.

- Names of Aboriginal origin or with a historical background are preferred.

- Names acknowledging the multicultural nature of our society are encouraged.

- The changing of long-established place names is avoided except where necessary to avoid ambiguity, offence or duplication.

- Place names may perpetuate the names of eminent persons, particularly those of early explorers, settlers and naturalists. Names of persons should normally only be given posthumously though at times the Board, at its discretion, may approve a feature name that honours a living person whose contribution to the local community has been of outstanding benefit to the community.

- Long and clumsily constructed names and those composed of two or more words are avoided.

- The preference is to have different parts of the same topographical feature, such as a stream or a mountain range, known by the same name.

- The naming of forks, arms and branches of a river as North Branch and South Branch is not favoured. Generally, it is preferable to assign independent names to river branches.

- The use of cardinal points of the compass as a prefix or suffix to an existing name is not favoured. However, well-established names that carry such a prefix or suffix may be approved.

- Where names have been changed by long-established local usage, it is not usually advisable to attempt to restore the original form but to adopt that which is sanctioned by general usage.

- The possessive form should be avoided whenever possible without destroying the sound of the name or changing its descriptive application. Where it remains, for example, Howes Valley, it should be written without the apostrophe.

- The use of hyphens in connecting parts of names should be avoided.

- Names considered likely to give offence are not approved.

Clearly, considerable thought underpins today's guidelines regarding naming conventions. While never undermining these, this book nonetheless celebrates the somewhat random, occasionally quixotic nature of historical custom in Australia, in particular the human qualities that emerge in the stories behind the names.

Indigenous history and place names

It will be immediately apparent that the place names with which this work is concerned relate to the colonial period of Australia's history — the last 220 years approximately. This means that far less attention is given than would have been liked to indigenous names. A number of reasons account for this restriction.

The most important is the notorious unreliability of the supposed Aboriginal names used by early settlers. Often the actual original name was changed by the settlers when it was written down for the first time. Some sounds that must have been unusual to an English-speaking person were heard and subsequently recorded as approximations rather than replications of the indigenous names.

While the indigenous peoples had their own place names, these were not written down. In fact, the map is derived from the land. Hence the name of the book *The Land is a Map*, which is about the naming conventions of indigenous Australia (Hercus, Hodges & Simpson 2002).

Variations among different Aboriginal languages and dialects spoken in the same area sometimes compounded difficulties in recording indigenous names. For example, the name of the town of Bli Bli in south-eastern Queensland is considered by some to be a corruption of 'billai billai', supposedly a local Gubbi Gubbi word for 'swamp oak', which is a tree that grows along the banks of the local Maroochy River. Then again, some say that 'bli bli' derives from a local word meaning 'twisted stream'.

A combination of factors contributes to the unreliability. They include mishearing, anglicisation, conversion of sound to a written form using the alphabet of a different language, the influence of multiple dialects, and sadly, insufficient interest in and investigation of local culture by the settling and naming populations. As well, different languages and peoples had different conventions of place naming.

A few examples are illustrative. In the case of Innaloo, the area was originally known by the Aboriginal name 'Njookenbooroo' but this proved too difficult for settlers to pronounce. An alternative name was sought and 'Innaloo', reputed to be the name of a local Aboriginal woman, was chosen.

Yunderup is another example of what can happen in the processes of anglicising an indigenous word. 'Yunderup' is an Aboriginal word derived from 'Yoondooroop', the name of one of the islands in the Murray delta. In the late nineteenth century, during a planned subdivision of land, the Surveyor-

General approved the Aboriginal name spelt as 'Yundurup', to allow it to conform to the orthographical conventions of the Royal Geographical Society, in which native names having the sound 'oo' were spelt with a 'u' (as in 'Zulu'). The townsite was gazetted as 'Yundurup' in 1898, but over the years common usage converted the pronunciation to 'Yunderup', and this spelling was approved in 1973.

Another complicating factor derives from the untranslatability of some words from one language into another. Bill Noble cites the research findings from place names in northern Queensland.

> As with personal names, place names too have important meanings, but not meanings that are always translatable through linguistic analysis. The name of [the township of] Borroloola ... refers to a lagoon and a stand of ghost gum trees ... Many non-indigenous people believe the name to mean 'the place of many paperbarks', but such a belief is drawn more from the need of such people to want names to have meaning regardless of whether or not the meaning is correct. In [the language of the] Yanyuwa, the name would be better rendered as Burrulula and is said to have no meaning, other than that the Hill Kangaroo spirit ancestor ... placed the lagoon and the trees there as he travelled and named the place.
>
> Noble 2004

The untranslatability is no surprise when we consider that indigenous ways of place naming are often entirely different from the European way. For example, 'in many indigenous Australian communities . . . people take their name from places, rather than bestow their names on places' (Simpson 2003). Furthermore, the names tend to make sense within the context of a cultural story, rather than in isolation. Then again, insisting that names mean something may itself be fallacious. As Appleton writes, 'What, for instance, does "London" mean?' (1992).

In researching this book, I experienced a number of jarring incongruences. There is the awful irony of the fact that contempt for the peoples from whom the lands were stolen sits alongside the preservation of the names of the land and the landscape. As

Bruce Pascoe puts it, 'It's peculiar, eerie, to have the names but almost none of the people' (2003).

Then there's the fact of the number of indigenously inspired place names around Australia and the absence of knowledge about or interest in indigenous history. While this has shifted over the last two decades (McKenna 2002), the awareness has mostly come too late — dispossession, dispersal and death have meant an irreversible loss of the people, much of their culture and many of their languages.

The incongruence was compounded for me by the fact that authenticated or not, most indigenous-sounding names point to topographical features of the landscape. While this of course reflects the deep connection of peoples to their lands, it also highlights other absences. It's a sad metaphor for the dispossession of a people that their presence is remembered so widely by topographically-oriented words taken or adapted from their languages but precious little about what lies beneath. There is more to the world of Australia's indigenous peoples than the surface level of their physical environment, and yet it is this that overwhelmingly dominates the place name 'borrowings'.

It is out of respect for indigenous history that I have concentrated less on indigenous names than on the names and stories that followed the paths of the settlers. I chose the easier of the two tasks, being aware of the enormity of what is not known, as well as the ways in which the processes of historical recording can extinguish and obliterate, creating in Mark McKenna's evocative words 'a geology of fable'.

ABC Range (SA) — Lettered hills

These South Australian mountains are known as the ABC Range as there are reputed to be twenty-six separate hills.

Aberdeen (NSW) — A friend in high places

Named in 1838 after George Hamilton-Gordon, 4th Earl of Aberdeen, a distinguished statesman and scholar, the name having been suggested by an ex-member of the British Parliament, a friend of the Earl.

Adaminaby (NSW) — Believe it or not

A story, possibly apocryphal, relates how a German settler gave a mine to his wife, whose name was Ada, and he said, 'Ada's mine it be'. Another version of the naming claims it comes from an Aboriginal word meaning 'camping' or 'resting place'.

Adelaide (SA) — Geometric plan

The capital of South Australia was named after Prinzessin Adelheid Amalie Luise Therese Carolin, who was born in 1792 in the castle of Meiningen, Germany. In 1818 she married the heir to the British throne, at which time the spelling of her name was changed from Adelheid to Adelaide. In 1830 William was crowned King William IV of Great Britain, and Adelaide became Queen. The town of Adelaide was meticulously planned from the start, making it unusual among Australian cities. The designer, Colonel William Light, the colony's first Surveyor-General, planned the city along a clearly defined grid pattern with the two major centres — Adelaide Central and North Adelaide — surrounded by parks. The result gives a neat geometric impression of a square figure eight. Adelaide's early years were clouded by economic problems and conflict, but by the 1840s, it started to make good on its promise. (See Nicknames, p. 146, Royalty, p. 175.)

Adelong (NSW)   Plain rivers

This small town near Tumut with a creek running through it is said to be derived from an Aboriginal word meaning 'along the way'. However, according to other sources, the meaning is 'a plain with a creek running through' or 'a plain with a river'.

Advale (QLD)   Lost and not found

Said to be originally called Ad's Veil after an incident when a woman travelling with her husband in 1870 lost her veil while crossing a creek. Later when the railway line reached the township, the name was changed to 'Advale'.

Afghan Rocks (WA)   Safe carriage

An unconfirmed story exists that the name comes from the fact that Afghans were commonly used as carriers when the product was liquor because they could be trusted with it — their religion prohibited alcohol.

Agnes Banks (NSW)   Remember Mum

Named after early settler Andrew Thompson's mother, when Thompson was granted 78 acres on the banks of the Nepean River in 1804, by Governor Philip Gidley King.

Ajana (WA)   An axe to grind

The name of this farming town in the wheat belt north of

Northampton is believed to be derived from 'Ajano', the Aboriginal name for the area around nearby Barrel Well. A different source states the name is derived from the word 'Ngatjana' or 'Ngajna', an Aboriginal word meaning 'mine', suggesting that stone axes would be quarried at such places. (See Aboriginal Names, p. 11.)

Alawa (NT)   Bombing leaves a mark

Alawa is one of Darwin's northern suburbs and was constructed in the late 1960s. The name comes from an Aboriginal tribe who inhabited an area on the southern tributaries of the Roper River. The street names in Alawa commemorate the residents and workers at the old Post Office who were killed in the bombing of Darwin by the Japanese in 1942.

Albany (WA)   Playing favourites

A city named after Frederick, Duke of Albany and York, the favourite son of King George III. (See Royalty, p. 175.)

Alberton (VIC)   The consort

Named after Prince Albert, Queen Victoria's consort, in 1842. Originally the township consisted of two communities known as Alberton and Victoria, divided by Victoria Street. It wasn't until the 1880s that the township became known solely as Alberton. (See Royalty, p. 175.)

Albury (NSW)   Losing a letter

A border town between NSW and Victoria, named after Aldbury in Hertfordshire, and later losing its 'd'.

Alectown (NSW)   Three for the price of one

This place name is derived not from one Alec but from three: the Alexanders Cameron, Patton and Whitelaw, three prospectors in the gold boom of the 1860s.

Alexandrina (SA)   Little princess

Named after Princess Alexandrina, who later became Queen Victoria. (See Royalty, p. 175.)

Alice Springs (NT)　　　The woman behind the man

This outback city in the centre of the continent is affectionately known as 'The Alice'. It was named after the nearby springs, which were reputed to be named after the wife of Sir Charles Todd (Lady Alice Todd), the then Postmaster-General of South Australia and the driving force behind the building of the Overland Telegraph. (See Nicknames, p. 146.)

Alkimos (WA)　　　Greek tragedy

A coastal suburb of Perth, it was named after the Greek freighter *Alkimos,* which ran aground nearby in 1963. (See Ship Names, p. 183.)

Alleys Hill (NSW)　　　Shipping magnate

This area was named after Captain Ben Alley who was associated with ships and trading for forty-three years prior to his death in 1911. During this time he was in charge of both sailing and steam-driven vessels.

Alligator Rivers (NT)　　　Crocs not 'gators

In 1818 Captain Phillip Parker King mistakenly identified crocodiles as alligators infesting the marshes along the banks of the East, South and West Alligator rivers; hence the somewhat inappropriate name. These days the area is prized for its barramundi fishing rather than its non-existent alligators. (See Mistakes and Apocrypha, p. 139.)

Allynbrook (NSW)　　　Named for home

Named by early Welsh settlers after the River Alyn near the border of North Wales and England.

Alpha (QLD)　　　Poets rule

A small township that calls itself the 'gateway to the west', officially gazetted in 1885. Many of its streets honour English poets, for example, Milton, Dryden, Byron, Tennyson, Burns, and Kendall Streets. According to local folklore, the only street in town not named after a poet was the main one, Shakespeare

Street, which is said to be named after the local publican, George Shakespeare. (See Literary Names, p. 123.)

Amaroo (NSW)   Red, muddy and beautiful

This locality, like the pastoral stations of the same name that once covered the area, takes its name, apparently, from an Aboriginal word for 'a lovely place'. Alternative meanings given are 'red mud' and 'rain'.

Ambleside (SA)   Return to sender

Many Germanic place names in Australia were changed in 1917 because of anti-German sentiment. Ambleside was the new name given to Hahndorf by a committee following a letter from England postmarked Ambleside. In 1937, however, it reverted to its original name. (See Changed Names, p. 30, German Names, p. 83.)

Amen Corner (SA)   Voice of God

About 6 kilometres south of Stokes Bay, on Kangaroo Island, Amen Corner was so named because it was a meeting place for the collection of mail, where one of the early settlers used to give a religious talk.

Anakie (VIC)   Small hill

Derived from the traditional name 'nganaki yawa' meaning 'small hill'. (See Aboriginal Names, p. 11.)

Andamooka (SA)   Bone of contention

The name means 'large waterhole' in the local Aboriginal language of the Kokatha people and is linked to the powerful bone of Aboriginal lore and retribution. The Aborigines believed that if they had this bone (it was a small kangaroo bone) pointed at them they would die.

Anglesea (VIC)   Tourist dollar

Swampy Creek became Anglesea when it was considered that the original name was unattractive enough to deter tourism. (See Changed Names, p. 30.)

ANTIQUITY

As the place names below illustrate, antiquity has been an ample inspiration across this vast continent. For details of the origins of place names, refer to the main text. For other names from antiquity, see Tasmanian Names, p. 199.

Place name	State/territory	Geographical feature
Arcadia Vale	NSW	a town
Bethany	SA	a town
Beulah	VIC	a town
Ithaca	QLD	a creek and suburb
Jacobs Well	QLD	a waterhole
Jericho	QLD	a tiny township
Jordan River	QLD	a small river
Lake Galilee	QLD	a lake
Mannahill	NSW	a run
Mount Ararat	VIC	a mountain
Nebo	QLD	a town
Palmyra	WA	a suburb
Proserpine	QLD	a town and shire
The Twelve Apostles	VIC	a set of stone stacks and pillars rising straight out of the sea
Walhalla	VIC	an old gold-mining town

Antwerp (VIC)   Belgian connection

A tiny town 356 kilometres north-west of Melbourne. The first settler, Horatio Ellerman, named his property 'Antwerp' after the city in Belgium where he was born. (See Nostalgia, p. 151.)

Anzac Hill (NT)   Tribute to the troops

The hill overlooking the town of Alice Springs, named as many places were, after the Australian forces sent to fight in World War I. (See War Names, p. 218.)

Appin (NSW)   Memories of home
Located on the fringe of the south-western urban sprawl of
Sydney, Appin was named in 1811 by Governor Macquarie
after a small coastal village in Argyllshire in Scotland where his
wife was born. (See Nostalgia, p. 151.)

Aramac (QLD)   Starting out as carved initials
Aramac is the name of a creek, town and shire in Queensland.
In the 1850s Robert Ramsay Mackenzie was exploring the
area and while there, he carved 'R R Mac' on a tree. This
was later found by the explorer William Landsborough who
adapted the initials to 'Aramac' and named the creek after it.
Later, the town and the shire that developed in the area took
the same name.

Arcadia Vale (NSW)   Paradise
A name calling on Greek mythology meaning an idyllic rustic
paradise, Arcadia Vale was originally called 'Arcadia', the 'Vale'
being added to avoid confusion with another Arcadia also in
NSW. (See Antiquity, p. 6.)

Archipelago of the Recherche (WA)   French ship
Comprising more than a hundred little islands as well as many
reefs and rocks, the Archipelago of the Recherche was named
by the French navigator d'Entrecasteaux who happened upon
them in 1792. Although not the first person to note them, he
was the first to name them, after his ship the *Recherche*.

Ardath (WA)   Prophet
A townsite named after a prophet mentioned in the second book
of the Apocrypha, *Edras*, or from the novel *Ardath, the Story of
a Dead Past* by Marie Corelli. (See Literary Names, p. 123.)

Arnhem Land (NT)   Older than a Dutch ship
The north-eastern corner of the Northern Territory, now an
Aboriginal reserve, this area has a long history of exploration
going back some 40000 to 50000 years. It was named by

Matthew Flinders after the Dutch ship *Arnhem*, which explored the coast in 1623.

Artarmon (NSW)   Literary Greeks

The name could be a corruption of the Greek name Artemon. There were at least five Greeks with the name Artemon, all of whom had some literary connection. Coincidentally, the modern suburb of Artarmon is home to quite a number of businesses involved in books and publishing. This allusion may well be apocryphal as evidence exists to confirm that Artemon was named by William Gore, who was Provost Marshall to Governor William Bligh, after his home in Ireland. Then again, perhaps the original Artemon in Ireland is an echo of the Greek Artemon. (See Literary Names, p. 123, Nostalgia, p. 151.)

Ashbourne (SA)   Literary village

Named after a village in Derbyshire, England, where Thomas Moore wrote the poem 'Lalla Rookh'. (See Literary Names, p. 123.)

Attack Creek (NT)   Bad news

At this place, on 26 June 1860, J McDouall Stuart and his companions abandoned their attempt to cross Australia

---

ARTISTS

The streets of Milgate Park estate in Doncaster East, Victoria, honour our landscape painters.

Buvelot Wynd	Lambert Place
Dobel Place	Landscape Place
Dowling Grove	Nolan Close
Drysdale Place	Roberts Way
Frater Court	Streeton Lane
Heysen Grove	Watling Terrace

from south to north due to exhaustion, lack of provisions, starving horses and attacks by Aboriginal people. (See War Names, p. 218.)

Auburn (SA)   A poet is born here
This is the birthplace of the poet C J Dennis, author of *The Songs of a Sentimental Bloke* (1915). (See Literary Names, p. 123.)

Augusta (WA)   Royal influence
A town named in honour of Princess Augusta Sophia, the second daughter of King George IV and Queen Charlotte. (See Royalty, p. 175.)

Australia   Down under
Long before explorers discovered continental Australia, it was referred to as 'terra australis incognita' — or 'the unknown south land'. In fact, it began appearing on European maps from the fifteenth century. But even before then it existed as an imaginary continent, first introduced by Aristotle and later expanded by Ptolemy, a first-century AD Greek geographer.

The belief was revived during the Renaissance, with cartographers and scientists continuing to argue that a large landmass needed to exist in the south to counterbalance the Northern Hemisphere. When the Dutch landed on the West Australian coast in 1616, that part of Australia became known as New Holland. Later Abel Tasman charted some of the southern coastline, and referred to Tasmania as Van Diemen's Land. In 1770 Captain James Cook named the entire east coast of Australia New South Wales, while the United Kingdom called the land 'terra nullius' (empty land, land of nothing, inhabited by no one), a cruel denial of the existence of indigenous Australians, foreshadowing their dispossession.

It wasn't until Matthew Flinders became the first European to circumnavigate the entire continent that the country became known as Australia. Flinders presented his book of his voyages to

Lachlan Macquarie, Governor of New South Wales, accompanied by a set of maps entitled *General Chart of Terra Australis or Australia* in 1817. By the late 1820s, the name Australia was in common usage.

Avoca River (VIC)   Sweet poem

Named after the 'Sweet Vale of Avoca', a poem by Thomas Moore. (See Literary Names, p. 123.)

Ayr (QLD)   Scottish inspiration

Named after a place of the same name in Scotland. (See Nostalgia, p. 151.)

ABORIGINAL NAMES

The continent of Australia has been inhabited for over 40000 years. By the time the first Europeans arrived, the many Aboriginal communities and language groups had already named most of the major and minor features in the Australian landscape. With European exploration and expanding settlement came a major set of new names, often in ignorance of the fact that established names already existed. Often Aboriginal languages named apparently minor features of the landscape that English speakers had overlooked. The newcomers had less need to be so intimately knowledgeable about the land, which no doubt contributed to the lack of significance they gave many features that already had indigenous names.

At the same time, settlers must have realised, too, that they needed to use the local vocabularies. 'The landscape of Australia was so foreign to the newcomers that the English vocabulary would often not suffice in describing it . . . thus, the colonists utilized indigenous words as a type of vernacular mapping technique for finding themselves in the bush' (Kostanski 2003).

Despite the European custom of renaming, a massive number of place names around Australia have indigenous origins, even if many of the languages of the original peoples are no longer or not currently in daily use. Often what remains today is a version of the original word — picked up by Europeans who interpreted what they thought they heard locals calling local landmarks. Often their words were valued for their pleasant or strange sounds and once adopted lost their connection to their context. Another factor to consider is that many names were the outcome of conversations between early settlers and local Aborigines, and the names may reflect linguistic or cultural misunderstandings and, in some cases, an Aboriginal person's sense of humour. For example, Coonamble (NSW) is said to be adapted from a local word, 'gunambil', said to mean 'full of dirt'.

The process of verification of Aboriginal derivations is extraordinarily difficult. One reason is that those responsible for recording the early names often did so unreliably and usually did not note the language from which the place name was derived. Place names can be from the country they appear in but can also be transferred from another country. Thus some names in the table below are associated with a specific language and others are not. As a consequence, given the less than perfect records, today many apparent Aboriginal names are imprecise, needing to be qualified by terms like 'thought to be derived from' or 'a version of' an indigenous word (Kostanski 2003). In general, even names based on long-accepted translations from Aboriginal languages are to be treated with caution.

Place name	State/ territory	Origin
Ajana	WA	Believed to be derived from 'Ajano', the Aboriginal name for the area around nearby Barrel Well. A different source states the name is derived from the word 'Ngatjana' or 'Ngajna', an Aboriginal word meaning 'mine', suggesting that stone axes would be quarried at such places.
Anakie	VIC	Derived from the traditional name 'nganaki yawa', meaning 'small hill'.
Balgowlah	NSW	An Aboriginal word meaning 'north harbour'.
Bondi	NSW	Derived from the local word 'boondi', meaning 'noise made by sea wave breaking on beach'.
Bonegilla	VIC	Derived from the traditional name 'bongella', meaning 'small island(s)'.
Brindabella	ACT	Derived from an Aboriginal word meaning 'two kangaroo rats'.

Place name	State/ territory	Origin
Ceduna	SA	A corruption of the local Aboriginal word 'chedoona', meaning 'a place to sit down and rest'.
Coober Pedy	SA	Said to be a translation of the Aboriginal word for 'boy' (or uninitiated man or white man) and 'pedy', meaning 'hole' or 'rock hole'. Together, the name means 'white fellow's hole in the ground'.
Coolum Beach	QLD	Derived from the Gabi-gabi language, 'gulum' or 'kulum' meaning 'blunt' or 'headless', referring to the shape of Mount Coolum, which has no peak. Other meanings have also been suggested, such as 'bear', 'fat snake' and 'death adder'.
Curl Curl	NSW	Drawn from a local word, 'curial curial', meaning 'river of life'.
Dimbulah	QLD	A Muluridji Aboriginal word for 'long waterhole'.
Ettamogah	NSW	Popularly considered to be derived from a local Aboriginal word for 'let's have a drink', which may or may not be related to the vineyards in the area.
Gabbin	WA	Derived from 'gabbabin', thought to be a local Aboriginal Nyoongar word relating to water.
Ginninderra	ACT	Originally the name of a creek that flows through Belconnen but now also another suburb, its name derived from an Aboriginal word meaning 'sparkling like the stars'.
Gunbower	VIC	From an Aboriginal word 'gambowra', thought to mean 'twisting'.
Illawarra	NSW	This was the native name for the area that early explorers and settlers referred to as the 'five islands district'.

Aboriginal Names

Place name	State/territory	Origin
Jerilderie	NSW	From a Wiradhuri word for 'reedy place'.
Katamatite	VIC	From an Aboriginal word 'catamateet', meaning 'of local creek'.
Killara	NSW	A local word meaning 'permanent, always there'.
Laanecoorie	VIC	From two Aboriginal words — 'languy' meaning 'resting place' and 'coorie' meaning 'kangaroo'.
Molonglo	ACT	Thought to be derived from an Aboriginal word meaning 'like the sound of thunder'.
Mooloolaba	QLD	Derived either from 'mulu' or 'mullu', an Aboriginal word for 'black snake', meaning 'place of black snakes' ('muluaba'). Alternatively, derived from 'mula', which means 'fishing nets'; hence the belief that it means 'place of the snapper fish'.
Nambucca	NSW	Derived from the word 'ngambugka' in the Gumbaynggirr language meaning 'crooked river' or 'entrance to the waters'. It is possible that the phrase 'ngambaa baga-baga' was corrupted by white settlers to 'Nambucca'.
Omeo	VIC	An Aboriginal word for 'mountains'.
Peregian Beach	QLD	An Aboriginal word for 'emu'.
Pingaring	WA	Derived from the name of a nearby spring.
Quambatook	VIC	A traditional word for 'rat'.
Suggan Buggan	VIC	The traditional Aboriginal name is 'soogin boogun', meaning 'ground'.
Taronga (Zoo)	NSW	An Aboriginal word for 'sea view'.
Toowoomba	QLD	A local Aboriginal word 'tchwampa' (or 'chhwoom' or 'toowooba'), meaning 'place where melons grow' or 'water sit down'.

Place name	State/territory	Origin
Undera	VIC	Derived from an Aboriginal word meaning 'fat'.
Wadderin	WA	Derived from the Aboriginal name of a nearby hill, the word is similar to another one meaning 'doe kangaroo'.
Wahroonga	NSW	An Aboriginal word meaning 'our home'.
Warrandyte	VIC	A combination of the Aboriginal words 'warran', meaning 'to throw', and 'dyte', meaning 'the object aimed at'.
Yackandandah	VIC	This is the traditional Aboriginal name, derived from the word 'tackan', meaning 'something extraordinary'.
You Yangs	VIC	This name comes from the Aboriginal words 'wurdi youang' or 'ude youang', meaning 'big mountain in the middle of a plain'.

B

Backstairs Passage (SA)   Private entrance

Named by Matthew Flinders who wrote, 'It forms a private entrance . . . to the two gulfs' — that is, Gulf St Vincent and Investigator Strait. (See Topography, p. 196.)

Baddaginnie (VIC)   Hungry

A rural locality with a small village, on mainly flat unforested country, this site was surveyed for settlement in 1857. Its name is believed to be derived from an expression meaning 'hungry', learned in Ceylon by the surveyor, and clearly on his mind as the survey team was low on food when it first arrived in the area.

Badger Creek (VIC)   Immortality in a bog

One version is that the place was named after a horse called 'Badger', owned by one of the pioneering settlers. Apparently, one day Badger became bogged in the creek, and the incident gave both the creek and the settlement the name. (See Horses, p. 95.)

Badger Head (TAS)   Mistaken identity

The origins of the name are obscure. One possibility is that early settlers confused local wombats with English badgers.

Another is that a horse named 'Badger', owned by one of the pioneering settlers, became bogged in the creek, and gave both the creek and the settlement their name. Another story has it that the name came from Charlotte Badger, who played an active role in hijacking a ship in the early days of settlement. (See Mistakes and Apocrypha, p. 139.)

Bagdad (TAS)   Small library
Named after the city in *The Arabian Nights*, which, according to legend, was one of the two books carried by explorer-soldier Hugh Germain and his convict friend, Jorgen Jorgensen, in the early nineteenth century. The other book they carried was the Bible, and allegedly they named places alternatively from one source or the other. (See Literary Names, p. 123, Tasmanian Names, p. 199.)

Bakers Hill (WA)   Dropping a letter
Originally declared as Mount Baker in 1897, in honour of an early settler, it was changed to Baker's Hill in 1902 to avoid confusion with Mount Barker. The apostrophe was officially dropped in 1944. (See Changed Names, p. 30.)

Balcolyn (NSW)   Happy blend
Amalgam of the Scottish prefix 'Bal' and the name Colyn. (See Nostalgia, p. 151.)

Bald Hills (QLD)   Exposed
Two treeless hills amid scrub-covered plain, provided this name around 1871. (See Topography, p. 196.)

Baldivis (WA)   Honouring the boats
This suburb was part of the State Government's Group Settlement schemes implemented in the 1920s to alleviate unemployment. When the school building was completed, it was named 'Baldivis', itself coined by local settlers after the three ships that brought them to Western Australia in 1922 — the *Balranald*, the *Diogenes* and the *Jervis Bay*. (See Ship Names, p. 183.)

Balgowlah (NSW)   View from the north
An Aboriginal word meaning 'north harbour'. (See Aboriginal Names, p. 11, Nicknames, p. 146.)

Balhannah (SA)   Honouring the Hannahs
A township established by Scotsman James Turnbull Thompson, in the early 1840s. He chose the last part of the town name to honour his mother and sister who were both called Hannah. The first syllable is either a corruption of 'belle' for 'beautiful' or of the Gaelic 'bal', which means 'town'.

Balla Balla (WA)
A river near Port Hedland. (See Double Names, p. 101.)

Ballarat (VIC)   Fifteen minutes of democracy
Ballarat is said to be derived from the local Wathawurung language meaning 'resting or camping place'. An hour's drive west of Melbourne, it is best known for its early history at the time of the gold rush in the mid 1850s. In 1854, a 15-minute rebellion, called the Eureka Stockade, made its way into the history books. It was the only armed civil uprising against the government in Australia's history. All miners on Victorian goldfields were expected to pay a licensing fee in advance. Discontented, the miners developed the slogan 'no taxation without representation'. On 29 November 1854, they gathered in their thousands at Bakery Hill and defiantly burnt their licences. A few days later, after grouping together behind a stockade, they were confronted by the soldiers. Twenty-two miners and six soldiers were killed. The event has remained deeply engraved in Australia's history. Its immediate outcome was that the licence fee was replaced by a miner's right. Holders of a miner's right were given the right to vote, so Eureka is remembered for its role in the development of democracy in Australia.

Ballidu (WA)   Compromise
The name Ballidu is the result of a compromise between the Department of Lands and Surveys and local residents, the former

wanting to name the place Duli, after nearby Duli Rockhole, and local residents wanting Balli Balli after a nearby soakage. The name 'Ballidu' was gazetted in 1914.

Bandiana (VIC)   Legs on flat ground

Bandiana, consisting mainly of a military establishment, is immediately south-east of Wodonga in north-eastern Victoria. According to early records, which have since been described as 'fanciful', the name is linked to an Aboriginal woman with bandy legs. A later authority claims the name is derived from an Aboriginal word meaning 'hill', which may be just as fanciful, as Bandiana is located on flat ground, although overlooked by hills to the north and the south.

Bapaume (QLD)   Bloodstains

A township near Stanthorpe named after a World War I battlefield in France, where Australian soldiers had fought. (See War Names, p. 218.)

Barossa (SA)   A touch of Spain

The Barossa Valley was named in 1837 by South Australia's first Surveyor-General, Colonel William Light and was first settled in 1842 by English and German settlers. The name comes from Barossa, in Spain.

Basket Range (SA)   A basket in the hills

Basket Range is one of a number of historical towns in the Adelaide Hills. Many stories exist to explain the name. The most convincing relates to the timber cutters who used to require a licence, and a licence inspector named Basket was reportedly stationed there.

Bass Strait (TAS)   Water all around

In a trip to prove that Van Diemen's Island was indeed an island, Matthew Flinders honoured his co-explorer George Bass, the ship's doctor he had met on their first trip together, sailing to Australia on the *Reliance*. (See Exploration Names, p. 66.)

Batchelor (NT)   Playing politics
Named after a South Australian and federal politician, Egerton Batchelor. (See Dignitaries, p. 60.)

Bathurst (NSW)   Colonial connections
Named after Earl Bathurst, British Secretary of State for the Colonies. (See Dignitaries, p. 60.)

Battery Point (TAS)   Protection
An historical inner suburb on the east side of Hobart fronting onto the Derwent River, Battery Point has the reputation of being the most complete colonial village in Australia with a lot of the buildings dating back to the 1830s and 1840s. It had its beginnings in about 1804 when the area belonged to Reverend Bobby Knopwood. Because of the battery of guns set up on the promontory to protect the citizens of Hobart, the settlement was known as Battery Point very early. However, the guns were never fired in anger. At one time the name was changed to East Hobart but this proved unpopular and was soon reverted.

Bay of Rest (WA)   Happy ending
Named thankfully by Captain Phillip Parker King, when the cutter *Mermaid*, after three days of dangerous battling against wind and sea, came to a safe anchorage in this bay. (See Topography, p. 196.)

Bay of Waterloo (SA)   Napoleon's demise
Named to commemorate the British victory over the French at Waterloo. (See War Names, p. 218.)

Beardy Plains (NSW)   A hairy reputation
Named in the 1830s after two stockmen called Duval and Chandler, who had an intimate knowledge of the region and were notable for their long black beards. Newcomers searching for suitable locations to establish their stations were advised to consult the 'beardies'. Beardy River and Beardy Waters are other place names in the same area.

Beauty Point (TAS)   What you see is what you get

While this place name seems to be a transparent label for a lovely spot on the landscape, in fact a local resident named it after a landowner's cow called 'Beauty', which was found dead on the point. (See Tasmanian Names, p. 199, Topography, p. 196.)

Beecroft (TAS)   The importance of time

This is a peak in Tasmania named by the early surveyor Henry Hellyer who had the habit of naming peaks after the day he climbed them, for example, St Valentine's Peak, Mayday and Sunday. But Mayday had to be changed because of the possible confusion with the international distress call. The new name was Beecroft.

Belli Park (QLD)   A man and his horse

The locality of Belli Park is believed to be named after a favourite horse, which died there in 1867, belonging to Jardine, a surveyor, who worked the road from Gympie to Brisbane. (See Horses, p. 95.)

Bells Mountain (NSW)   Not the telephone bell

Named after the explorer Lieutenant Archibald Bell. (See Exploration Names, p. 66.)

Bennett Springs (SA)   Honouring the horse

Named by J McDouall Stuart in 1861 after the death of one of his horses that had been with him on an earlier expedition. (See Horses, p. 95.)

Bethany (SA)   Fertility

From the Bible, it means 'a fertile place'. (See Antiquity, p. 6.)

Beulah (SA)   God said

Isaiah 62:4: 'Thou shalt no more be termed Forsaken; neither shall thy land anymore be termed Desolate: but thou shalt be called Hephzibah, and thy land Beulah; for the Lord delighteth in thee, and thy land shall be married.' (See Antiquity, p. 6.)

Bicheno (TAS) — Early reconciliation

Sealers and whalers called this spot on the north-eastern coast of Tasmania 'Waub's Harbour' after an Aboriginal woman called Waubedebar, who rescued two men from drowning. She died in 1832 and her tombstone reads, 'Erected in her memory by a few of her white friends'. The name 'Bicheno' came from the popular Colonial Secretary of Van Diemen's Land between 1842 and 1851, James Ebenezer Bicheno.

Big Wills Flat (NSW) — One size too small

A flat on Jacqua Creek near Goulburn, the name dates back to the mid-nineteenth century. Legend has it that an old and unwell pioneer known as Big Will dug his own grave and lined it with concrete. Deciding his time had come, he laid himself out in the grave and found it too short. His searchers found him dead sitting up in the grave.

Billys Creek (NT) — They all died

Named after explorer Burke's favourite horse, which perished in the outback as did both Burke and Wills. (See Horses, p. 95.)

Binnaway (NSW) — Ears away

Supposedly named as a result of an incident when one Aborigine cut off another's ear and threw it away. (See Mistakes and Apocrypha, p. 139.)

Birdsville (QLD) — Birds of a feather

Birdsville is probably so named because of the many birds to be seen here, including seagulls that come from salt lakes more than 600 kilometres away. (See Topography, p. 196.)

Birdwood (SA) — Replacing the Prussian

This town in the Torrens Valley was named after Sir William Birdwood, an Australian General during World War I who led the Anzacs at Gallipoli. His name was an obvious choice when the World War I place names committee decided to replace the town's original name of Blumberg, probably named after the

Prussian town of the same name. (See War Names, p. 218.)

Birkdale (QLD)   Arboreal
In England, Birkdale is a contraction of Valley of the Birches. It is said that the name was given to this part of Queensland because the tea-trees in the area resembled the English birches in appearance. (See Topography, p. 196.)

Birthday Siding (SA)   Birthday gift
A siding 50 kilometres north-west of Port Augusta, it is so named because a John Bevis struck water when the stock was much in need of it — and it happened to be on his birthday. (See Special Days, p. 186.)

Black Head (NSW)   Optical illusion
Name given by Captain James Cook as he passed up the coast to the North Head, probably because in the afternoon sun, the place presents that appearance. (See Topography, p. 196.)

Blackheath (NSW)   Blackness all around
Blackheath was first named Hounslow Heath by Governor Lachlan Macquarie after that place in England. It was later renamed by him because of its 'black wild appearance', noted in his journal. (See Changed Names, p. 30.)

Blaxland (NSW)
Named after explorer Gregory Blaxland. (See Exploration Names, p. 66.)

Bli Bli (QLD)
A town near Maroochydore. (See Double Names, p. 101.)

Bondi (NSW)   Sounds of the sea
From the local Aboriginal word 'boondi', thought to mean 'noise made by sea wave breaking on beach'. (See Aboriginal Names, p. 11.)

Bonegilla (VIC)   Isles
Derived from the traditional name 'bongella', meaning 'small

island(s)'. (See Aboriginal Names, p. 11.)

Boolaroo (NSW)   Immortalised in text
This town was depicted as 'Boomaroo' in the novels *Jack Rivers and Me* and *Good Mates* by Paul Radley. (See Literary Names, p. 123.)

Boomerang Park (NSW)   There and back
Quarry Hill Park in Raymond Terrace was renamed after the author and local businessman John Houlding who wrote under the name of 'Old Boomerang'. (See Literary Names, p. 123.)

Boono Boono (QLD)
A national park near Tenterfield. (See Double Names, p. 101.)

Bordertown (SA)   A border that's not a border
Perhaps because the border was once in dispute, this name became a misnomer, as it is 19 kilometres west of the actual border between South Australia and Victoria. (See Mistakes and Apocrypha, p. 139.)

Botany Bay (NSW)   Plants galore
Named by Captain James Cook in 1770 due to the great quantity of previously unknown plants found there. (See Topography, p. 196.)

Bottle and Glass (QLD)   A horsy story?
The origins of this place name have stirred a number of interpretations. One explanation is that a bottle and glass were carved into a tree at the top of a steep rise. A second says that a bottle and glass were found on the site. A third claims the name derives from two horses that used to help the regular horses in the Cobb and Co coach team. (See Horses, p. 95.)

Bountiful Island (QLD)   A new dish
Named by Matthew Flinders in 1872 after his men captured forty-six green turtles, a welcome addition to a year-long diet of salt pork and ship's biscuits. (See Topography, p. 196.)

Box Beach (NSW)   Squares
Named because the rocks flanking the beach appear to be in
a box-like shape. (See Topography, p. 196.)

Boys Town (NSW)   Second chance
Founded in 1939 and planned for the same purpose as Boys
Town in the United States — to give delinquent boys a second
chance. (See Topography, p. 196.)

Breakfast Creek (QLD)   A dry meal
A creek named in 1824 by a group of explorers, following a
memorable breakfast. The three explorers, John Oxley, Alan
Cunningham and Lieutenant Butler, accompanied by nine
boatmen and servants, travelling in two boats, left the brig
Amity moored off Redcliffe Point and rowed to the mouth of the
Brisbane River. From there the party travelled upstream to the
head of what Oxley called Sea Reach and camped overnight at
a grassy spot on the bank. Four local Aborigines came around
as they were setting up camp. The country was in the grip of
drought and a reedy swamp nearby linked to the river by a
creek had dried up. The only water they found was brackish
and undrinkable so they were compelled to use their water
cask that evening. The next day they again searched for fresh
water but without success. They ate a hasty (and dry) breakfast
near a dried-up creek, which they subsequently referred to
as Breakfast Creek. The custom of naming places, especially
creeks, after what was eaten or not eaten there is a feature in
Tasmania in places such as No Tea Creek, Muesli Creek and
Cornflakes Creek. (See Special Days, p. 186.)

Breakfast Point (NSW)   Sunny side up
Near Sydney, this place was named in 1788 with the arrival
of the First Fleet. Captain John Hunter set about charting the
harbour. His records indicate that on the fifth day, he sailed
west up a waterway that is now called the Parramatta River and
after about 10 kilometres he put ashore to have tea and a bite

to eat. This was his first charting and he named it Breakfast Point. (See Special Days, p. 186.)

Bribie Island (QLD)   Fish for freedom?

Place names in Australia are not often chosen, as this one was, to remember convicts. Some confusion, however, clouds the records. Bribie (or Brieby) may have been the man's nickname, a reference perhaps to the way he bought privileges from the authorities — apparently he supplied them with fish. He was a basket-maker and fish-trapper, and these skills seem to have made him a valued member of both white and Aboriginal societies. He took up with an Aboriginal woman and, when his term of sentence was about to expire, ran away to live permanently with her and her tribe on the island. Other convicts found sanctuary there as well. When a convict went missing, it was common to hear it said around Brisbane town that he was, 'Down with Bribie'. This became 'Down at Bribie' and so the island got its name. However, another suggestion is that the name derives from the original Aboriginal name for the island itself, 'Boorabee'. 'Bribie' was not the first white person to live with the natives on this island. Thomas Pamphlett and John Finnegan were found there in 1823 by John Oxley when he came looking for a site for a new convict settlement. They were two of a four-man crew who had sailed out of Sydney Heads to get cedar logs from the Illawarra district, but were blown way off course by a storm. One died at sea, but the three who were left eventually came ashore on Moreton Island, where they were befriended by the Aboriginal people. In the following year, Oxley found the other member of their crew, Richard Parsons, also on Bribie Island.

Bridgeman Downs (QLD)   Star appeal

This suburb of Brisbane is famous for its naming of streets after stars — the celestial kind. (See Stars, p. 188.)

Brindabella (ACT)   Not one, but two
The name associated with the mountain range that dominates the southern horizon of Canberra is derived from an Aboriginal word meaning 'two kangaroo rats'. (See Aboriginal Names, p. 11.)

Brisbane (QLD)   Salute the colonel
Brisbane was founded as the British penal station of 'Endinglassie' in 1824. Within ten years, it was declared a town and its name was changed to Brisbane in honour of the British astronomer and administrator Sir Thomas Brisbane (1773–1860), who was then governor of New South Wales, and had been an early explorer. Brisbane was opened to free settlers in 1842 and in 1859 it became the capital of the newly created colony of Queensland. The city's central business district is remarkably royalist. Some royally named streets are Anne, Adelaide, Elizabeth, Queen, Charlotte, Mary, Margaret and Alice. Running at right angles to these are George, Albert and Edward. (See Nicknames, p. 146, Royalty, p. 175, Stars, p. 188.)

Briseis Mine (TAS)   Horsy win
Named after the 1876 Melbourne Cup winner. (See Horses, p. 95.)

Broad Arrow (WA)   Follow me
The town of Broad Arrow was named around 1893 after a prospector scratched arrows in the dirt to make sure his mates could follow his trail.

Broke (NSW)   Going for broke
The name of this village in the Hunter Valley has nothing to do with financial affairs, as some assume, but rather honours Sir Charles Broke Vere, whom the namer, Surveyor-General Mitchell, knew as 'Broke'.

Broome (WA)   A pearl of a town
In the early 1870s pearl fishers began exploring this region

and in 1873 established a base. It was subsequently named Broome in honour of the then Governor of Western Australia, Fredrick N Broome. (See Dignitaries, p. 60.)

Brunswick (VIC)   Any royal is good enough
This suburb of Melbourne has a royal connection although exactly to whom is in dispute. It might be in honour of Princess Caroline of Brunswick (wife of King George IV) or of the marriage of Queen Victoria to Prince Albert of the royal house of Brunswick. (See Royalty, p. 175.)

Buccaneer Archipelago (WA)   Swashbuckling
Named by Captain Phillip Parker King after William Dampier, a swashbuckling buccaneer. The bay that fronts the islands was called Cygnet Bay after Dampier's vessel. (See Exploration Names, p. 66.)

Bugaldie (NSW)   From possums to music
'Bugaldi' was thought to be an Aboriginal word meaning 'blossoms damaged by possums'. The 'e' was added after World War II to commemorate soldiers who lost their lives: the pronunciation is 'bugle die'. (See War Names, p. 218.)

Bungle Bungle Range (WA)   What a bungle
The Bungle Bungle Range is in the Purnululu National Park in north-western Australia. The name 'Bungle Bungle' comes either from the corruption of an Aboriginal name for the area or from a misspelling of one of the common Kimberley grasses found here, bundle bundle grass. (See Double Names, p. 101, Pessimistic Names, p. 165.)

Burketown (QLD)   Passing through
This outback township on the edge of the Gulf of Carpentaria was named after the explorer Robert O'Hara Burke who, with his fellow explorer William John Wills, passed through the area in 1861. (See Exploration Names, p. 66.)

Burra (SA) One great or two

Located north of Adelaide, Burra was the site of Australia's first copper mines. 'Burra' derives from an Afghan word meaning 'great'. The early population was very diverse, including Afghan, Cornish, Irish, Welsh and Spanish people. The 'monster mine' that resulted from the discovery of copper in 1845 was, rather appropriately, called 'Burra Burra' ('great great'). The town became referred to as 'The Burra' or 'Burra', although for a time it was called 'Burra-of-the-five-towns' because the town is in fact a combination of half a dozen old townships (Kooringa, Redruth, Aberdeen, Hampton, Copperhouse and Lewychr), each with a distinctive character and history.

Bustard Bay (QLD) What's for dinner?

This place, which came to be known as the birthplace of Queensland, was given its name by Captain James Cook because his men shot a scrub turkey (bustard) for meat. (See Special Days, p. 186.)

Byron Bay (NSW) Poetic irony

When Captain James Cook sailed past in 1770, he named the Cape after a vice-admiral, not as is commonly thought, after the poet Lord Byron, who at that time was the vice-admiral's grandson and not yet famous. However, this anachronistic idea was perpetuated in the late nineteenth century when the streets of Byron Bay were laid out and named after famous poets, for example, Browning, Keats, Kingsley, Kipling, Marvell, Milton and Tennyson Streets. (See Literary Names, p. 123.)

CHANGED NAMES

Place naming, at least in theory, is a linear process of suggestion, discussion, consensus, and then the formal phase of gazetting, by which the proposed name becomes official. Sometimes this works relatively smoothly. On other occasions, a place name may be changed, and sometimes more than once, before a 'final' name is agreed on. We should probably not call this 'final' because, in theory at least, any name is subject to change in the future, provided the official processes are heeded. Usually, though, unless a name is offensive or confusing, it remains.

Name	State/ territory	Former name(s) and context
Bakers Hill	WA	Originally declared as Mount Baker in 1897, it was changed to Baker's Hill in 1902 to avoid confusion with Mount Barker. The apostrophe was officially dropped in 1944.
Blackheath	NSW	Governor Lachlan Macquarie first named this place Hounslow Heath and later renamed it Blackheath because of its 'black wild appearance'.
Carnegie	VIC	Originally called Rosstown and with the hope of a changed fortune became Carnegie.
Cherryville	SA	An historical town in the Adelaide Hills first called Sixth Creek but later renamed Cherryville.
Dayboro	QLD	Previously called Terror's Creek, allegedly after a prized Arab stallion (actually called 'Terah') that was said to instil terror in the locals. Later changed to Hamilton after a local farmer and then Dayboro, in 1919, after William Henry Day, a police magistrate in Brisbane.
Dover	TAS	Dover was earlier called Port Esperance, after one of the ships in Bruni D'Entrecasteaux's 1792 expedition. It was later renamed Dover after the English seaport of the same name.

Name	State/territory	Former name(s) and context
Garden Island	WA	This was earlier called Buache after the French geographer and historian Phillippe Buache.
Gudarra	WA	Gold was discovered here in 1892 and the place was known as Sore Foot Rush, a reference to the tired, limping diggers who first arrived. Then for unknown reasons, it changed to Paddington, and subsequently to Gudarra, of unknown meaning and source.
Hahndorf	SA	Named by German settlers in 1839, it changed to Ambleside during World War I, and reverted to Hahndorf in 1936.
Holbrook	NSW	Known by a number of names, in the 1850s it took the name Germanton. It was then changed during World War I.
Kingscote	SA	First named Angas but, after a dispute, it was renamed after Henry Kingscote.
Pemberton	WA	First known as Big Brook but this was not considered distinctive enough. The name Pemberton was used from 1916 and gazetted in 1925.
Swampy Creek	VIC	Swampy Creek became Anglesea when it was considered that the original name was unattractive enough to deter tourism.
Uluru	NT	The mammoth rock now known by its traditional name of Uluru was formerly known as Ayers Rock.
Yaroomba	QLD	First named Coronation Beach in 1953, it was changed to Yaroomba in 1961.

C

Cairns (QLD)   Let's hear it for the Guv

Named after Queensland's first Irish-born Governor, Sir William Wellington Cairns. Other names considered were Thornton, after the Collector of Customs in Brisbane, Dickson after the Colonial Treasurer of the time, Newport and Trinity Bay — the name given by Captain James Cook when he landed in the area on Trinity Sunday in 1770. (See Special Days, p. 186.)

Calista (WA)   Across the waves

The *Calista* arrived at the Swan River Colony with seventy-three passengers on 5 August 1829 under the command of Captain S Hawkins. (See Ship Names, p. 183.)

Calle Calle (NSW)

A bay near Eden. (See Double Names, p. 101.)

Cameron Corner (QLD)   A corner spot

Cameron Corner, in south-western Queensland, is the spot where the state borders of NSW, South Australia and Queensland converge. The Queensland part of the border here was pegged by surveyor John Cameron in 1880.

Canberra (ACT) A national meeting place

The capital of the nation, and the seat of Federal Government, is located in its own territory (the Australian Capital Territory) inland in south-eastern Australia. That it is halfway between Sydney and Melbourne is no accident: it was important that the selection of the site not favour, by proximity, either of those two large urban centres. In fact, the 1901 Constitution of the newly federated Australia required Parliament to choose a site at least 100 miles (160 kilometres) from Sydney. After a great deal of discussion, the site was chosen. The area was called 'Kamberra' by the Aboriginal people who'd been living there when British settlers first arrived. This name is thought to be derived from an indigenous word for 'meeting place', which, when you consider the nature and purpose of Federal Parliament, seems highly appropriate. However, recently, doubts about the indigenous origins of the name have been expressed, with the argument that there is no record of the word in any Aboriginal language. The settlers had been using this name — pronounced as two syllables, with the stress on the first syllable, as *Can*bra' — for about seventy-five years before it was officially named, in 1913. At the time when the decision was made to name the new site, a number of other suggestions were put forward, among them 'Federatia', 'New London', 'Kangaremu', 'Cookaburra', 'Wheatwoolgold', 'Caucus City', 'Democratica', 'Empire City', 'Eucalyptia' and 'Engirscot'. These names reflect the various political forces active at the time. There was a great deal of bickering and resentment over the costs involved (two suggestions for the new capital were 'Swindleville' and 'Gonebroke'). Many finally sighed with relief at noon on 12 March 1913 when the wife of the Governor-General, Lady Denham, mounted a crimson-draped platform and declared in a clear English voice, 'I name the capital of Australia, Canberra — the accent is on the Can'. (See Castle Names, p. 39, Nicknames, p. 146.)

NATIONAL CELEBRITIES

Canberra was planned as the nation's capital. Hence it is appropriate that more than any other city in the country, Canberra's suburbs and streets have been named for their national significance. Very often these are organised thematically, for example, by prime ministers or explorers or high achievers in other fields such as the arts or science. What emerges is a mosaic of the major and diverse contributors to national history. A trip to Canberra becomes a trip through history, as the small selection below illustrates.

Domain of national life	Suburb	Streets named after famous people
Artists	Weston	Folingsby Street, Namatjira Drive, Streeton Drive.
Explorers	Griffith	Hume Place, Hovell Street, Mitchell Street.
Film	Chapman	Beaumont Close, Chauvel Circle, Percy Close.
Inventions	Dunlop	Akubra Place, Ikara Close, Periscope Place, Splayd Close.
Medical profession	MacGregor	Florey Drive, Gibson Street, Weigall Place.
Mountains	Palmerston	Kosciusko Avenue, Sugarloaf Circle, Tamborine Close.
Public office	Deakin	Adelaide Avenue, Cairns Street, Napier Close.
Ships	Red Hill	Esperance Street, Fortitude Street, Reliance Street.
Social reformers	Oxley	Dalgarno Crescent, Hazel Smith Crescent, Kirby Place.
Writers	Garran	Astley Place, Becke Place, Dennis Street.

Cannon Hill (QLD)   Abstract art
A suburb of Brisbane named by the then Registrar-General who imagined that two fallen gum trees on his property looked like a couple of cannon poking out. The streets of Cannon Hill continue the theme of war, for example, Grenade Street, Shrapnel Street, Tomahawk Close, Bombery Street. Other war-related street names are found in the Brisbane suburb of Mount Gravatt, for example, Passchendale Street, Monash Street, Pozieres Road, Perrone Road. (See War Names, p. 218.)

Cape Adieux (SA)   Goodbye to all that
The point at which the French explorer Nicolas Baudin completed his charting of the Australian coast. (See French Names, p. 73.)

Cape Clear (VIC)   Not a cape at all
Named allegedly because a wagon driver got bogged down here and before going to get help he put up a notice to either warn others that the ground was soft or to warn them off touching his wagon. The words 'keep clear' were spelt 'kape klear'.

Cape Duquesne (VIC)   Hurrah for the duke
This cape near Portland is presumed to be named after the French naval commander Abraham Marquis Duquesne (1610–88), who helped France to overcome the Dutch naval supremacy of the time. (See French Names, p. 73, War Names, p. 218.)

Cape Inscription (WA)   Leaving messages
Dirk Hartog was the first European to set foot on the west coast of Australia and he left a pewter plate with an inscription giving details of his visit in 1616. The Cape was named in 1801 when a French captain visiting the island found that another Dutch voyager had called at the island in 1697 and had replaced Hartog's plate with another to commemorate the same event.

Cape Jervis (SA)   Family rules
Named by Matthew Flinders after the family name of the Earl of St Vincent, a Lord Commissioner of the Admiralty. (See Dignitaries, p. 60.)

Cape Marengo (VIC)   Inspiring battle
This name presumably honours Napoleon's victory against the Italians in the battle of Marengo in 1801. One of Napoleon's horses was also named after the battle. (See French Names, p. 73.)

Cape Montesquieu (VIC)   A French touch
On the Victorian coast, this name is one of eight given in the area by Nicolas Baudin, the commander of a major French scientific expedition that left Le Havre in France in 1800 with instructions to explore Van Diemen's Land and the southern coast of New Holland. As it turned out, English explorers, namely Matthew Flinders and Lieutenant James Grant, had beaten Baudin and left behind a swathe of English names on territory to which they lay claim. Baudin nonetheless left his mark on the naming of sites along the coastlines of Western Australia, South Australia and Tasmania. Less well known are the French names along the Victorian coast, such as Cape Montesquieu, which commemorates the name of the famous French philosopher and jurist, Charles Montesquieu (1689–1755). Other places are Cape Duquesne, Descartes Bay, Cape Volney, Cape Reamur, Cape Marengo, French Island and Venus Bay. Unlike the tendency of the English to name places after prominent English political figures, the French tended to name places after French writers, scientists and philosophers (Richards 2002). (See French Names, p. 73.)

Cape Naturaliste (WA)   Men behaving badly
In the early nineteenth century French Captain Nicolas Baudin was appointed to lead a scientific expedition to Australia, then known as 'New Holland'. He arrived at Cape Leeuwin on

27 May 1801 and from there traced the coast northwards to Geographe Bay, which he named after his ship. Scientifically, the trip was a success but it was awash with bad blood between the scientists and the seamen, itself epitomised by the feud between Baudin and the naturalist Francois Péron, who despised one another. At one time, Baudin became enraged by what he saw as the gross disobedience of his Sub-Lieutenant Picquet, who failed to reach shore as instructed, because of dangerous conditions. Peeved by this, Baudin named what is now Cape Naturaliste, 'Cape des Mecontents' (later anglicised to 'Cape of Discontent'). Baudin's foul mood continued and a few days later he expressed his displeasure by naming a cove 'Anse des Maladroits' (Incompetents Cove). When Péron later made the same voyage, he named a nearby promontory 'Point Picquet' after the seaman who had failed to reach shore as directed. He also removed the name 'Anse des Maladroits' from the map (Whittaker & Willesee 2002, pp. 204–07). (See French Names, p. 73.)

Cape Poivre (WA) — Spicy treat

Named after Pierre Poivre, who introduced East Indian spices to France, and is remembered eponymously ('le poivre' means 'pepper' in French). (See French Names, p. 73.)

Cape Reamur (VIC) — Honouring science

Named after a French scientist Réne Réaumur (1683–1757) who invented a now obsolete thermometer. The first 'u' of the original name has been dropped. (See French Names, p. 73.)

Cape Rose (WA) — Gutsy girl

Named after the young wife of a French sea captain, Louis-Claude de Freycinet, who led an expedition in 1817–20. Rose de Freycinet was secreted aboard the expedition disguised as a sailor and later wrote of her adventures in a journal that has been translated into English under the title *A Woman of Courage*. (See French Names, p. 73, Literary Names, p. 123.)

Cape Tribulation (QLD)   Landscaping trouble

On 10 June 1770 as Captain James Cook sailed along the northern Queensland coast in the *Endeavour*, passing a place that was known locally as 'Kuranjee' (an Aboriginal word for 'place of many cassowaries'), his vessel ran into a reef, only just avoiding a shipwreck. The next morning, the legend goes, he awoke in a particularly grumpy mood, and proceeded to assign some very negative names to the landscape around him. One such was Cape Tribulation. (See Pessimistic Names, p. 165, Special Days, p. 186.)

Cape Upstart (QLD)   In your face

Named after the massive granite headland that rises steeply from the sea. (See Topography, p. 196.)

Cape Volney (VIC)   Many talents

Believed to have been named after the French historian, travel writer and philosopher, Constantin Volney (1757–1820). (See French Names, p. 73.)

Carnegie (VIC)   Can't blame a town for trying

Carnegie is a residential suburb in south-eastern Melbourne on the railway line between Caulfield and Oakleigh. The district was originally known as Rosstown, named after William Ross, an entrepreneur who invested a lot of money in the construction of a railway line through the area. But the economic depression of the 1890s had a devastating effect on land speculation and the Rosstown railway was a failure. It appears that locals came to the view that a change of name may bring a change of fortune. In May 1909 the railway station was renamed Carnegie, allegedly because it was believed that this would attract funds for the community from the American Carnegie Foundation. This motive has never been documented but, in any case, the funds never eventuated and in the meantime, no better explanation has arisen for the name change to Carnegie. (See Changed Names, p. 30.)

Carseldine (QLD)   Relying on the young

Named after an illiterate immigrant whose true English family name was spelt 'Castledine' and was misspelt due to reliance

---

CASTLE NAMES

Many parts of Sydney developed with little forethought or planning. One exception to this is the suburb of Castlecrag. In early maps of the region, a formation of high rock, now called Tower Reserve, was known as Edinburgh Castle Rocks. In the 1920s, the whole area was renamed Castlecrag by the American architect Walter Burley Griffin, the winner of a competition to design and plan the construction of Canberra. Burley Griffin had a specific notion of how he wanted the area to be developed: 'No fences, no boundaries, no red roofs — I want Castlecrag built so that each individual can feel the whole of the landscape is his [sic]' (<http://farrer.riv.csu.edu.au/ASGAP/rise.html>). The plans for the development of the area were initially thwarted by the onset of the Great Depression, but in the end, Burley Griffin's innovative design, which was intended to 'follow the contours of the land', came to fruition, and a unique area of Sydney was created. As he wished, the streets and reserves of the promontory were named as parts of a castle. Some examples follow:

Casement Reserve	Castle-Haven Reserve
Corteille Reserve	Embrasure Reserve
Keep Reserve	Sortie Port
The Barbican	The Barricade
The Bastion	The Battlement
The Bulwark	The Citadel
The Palisade	The Parapet
The Rampart	The Redoubt
The Scarp	Turrett Reserve

on his young son. (See Mistakes and Apocrypha, p. 139.)

Cascade Bay (WA)   Vision of falling water

So named in 1838 by the commander of a British Navy survey ship, J Lort Stokes, who observed a large stream of water falling into the sea in a glittering cascade at the northern point of the bay. (See Topography, p. 196.)

Castlecrag (NSW)   Castle theme

In early maps of this region of Sydney, a formation of high rock, now called Tower Reserve, was known as 'Edinburgh Castle Rocks'. In the 1920s, the whole area was renamed 'Castlecrag' by the American architect Walter Burley Griffin, the winner of a competition to design and plan the construction of Canberra. Part of his plan for the development of Castlecrag was to name all the streets and reserves of the promontory after parts of a castle. (See Castle Names, p. 39.)

Caves Beach (NSW)   Hiding places

The naming of this place refers to the fact that there are large caves on the beach. (See Topography, p. 196.)

Ceduna (SA)   Welcome rest

This word is a corruption of the local Aboriginal word 'Chedoona', meaning 'a place to sit down and rest'. A traveller crossing the Nullarbor would have to agree. (See Aboriginal Names, p. 11.)

Cemetery Plain (NT)   Deathly image

This 48-kilometre wide area sprinkled with 'magnetic' anthills that lie due north and south was so named because the anthills stand up like monuments in a cemetery.

Cephissus Creek (TAS)   Exalted name

This creek was named after the river god of Greek mythology. (See Tasmanian Names, p. 199.)

Cervantes (WA)   Naming chain

Named after an island off the shore of Western Australia, which was named after the wreck of an American whaling ship, which, presumably, was named after the Spanish writer. (See Literary Names, p. 123.)

Chain of Ponds (SA)   Respite care
A small settlement dating back to the 1850s when the township was called a hamlet. It played a stopover role in the difficult trek across the Mount Lofty Ranges. The name came from a run of waterholes. (See Topography, p. 196.)

Channel Island (NT)   Out of sight, out of mind
Channel Island in Darwin Harbour is famous for its former leprosarium, or leper colony. There are the remains of numerous buildings and other infrastructure such as rusted galvanised iron, concrete slabs, partial wall and roof structures, collapsed ruins of huts and dwellings, and parts of the original road formations. The leprosarium is on the site of what had been a quarantine station, built in 1914 as one of four such stations used for first aid and accommodation for cases of actual 'quarantinable' diseases. In 1930, when a new quarantine station was opened elsewhere, Channel Island was converted into a leprosarium. The place is culturally significant in providing a unique view of a compulsorily isolated group of people who existed under extreme conditions. Interestingly, at a time when the rest of the world was modifying its compulsory isolation laws, Australia was doing the opposite.

Charleville (QLD)   Childhood memory
Named by the Government Surveyor, William Alcock Tully, after his boyhood home in Ireland. (See Nostalgia, p. 151.)

Chaucer Street (NSW)   Oblique lesson
A street in the Hunter Valley allegedly named so that the subdivider's children would come to know their English literature. (See Literary Names, p. 123.)

CORNISH NAMES

The County of Cornwall is located in the south-west corner of England, with an area of 3515 square kilometres and a population of nearly 500000. Despite its small size and population, Cornwall has had an important impact on Australia, especially in Victoria. For example, Captain James Cook named the place where land was first sighted, Point Hicks, after Lieutenant Zachary Hicks who made the sighting from the *Endeavour*. The second naming was Rame Head, named directly after that place in Cornwall where the *Endeavour* had set forth from England.

Emigration of the Cornish from England to Australia was triggered both by the economic conditions in England in the nineteenth century and the news that opportunities lay abroad. In particular, the Cornish were attracted to mining opportunities, for which they had an excellent reputation. Initially they were attracted to the copper mines in South Australia, to the extent that an area there was known as 'Little Cornwall'. Subsequently, the Cornish moved in large numbers to Victoria, encouraged by the discovery of gold.

Examples of Cornish names found in Victoria follow.

Places named after Cornwall and the Cornish people:
Fryerstown, Harveytown, Indigo, Newlyn and Tresco.

Houses named after Cornish towns and villages:
Camborne, Fowey, Mevagissey, Pendeen, Penryn, St Austell, St Ives and Troon.

Places named after someone with Cornish heritage:
Coode Island and Elizabeth Cove.

Places named after a Cornish saint:
St Erth, St Gwinear, St Ives, St Just Point, St Neot and St Phillack.

Places named after Cornish mining terminology:
Wheal Gawler and Wheal Kitty.

Cherry Gully (NSW)   The power of tut-tut

This name is an example of how local names given by local people are often overturned by officialdom. The original name was 'Sherry Gully', which derived from an incident when a bullock wagon broke a wheel, causing a keg of sherry to fall off and smash open. The authorities did not approve and the name was later changed to 'Cherry Gully'.

Cherryville (SA)   Pick of the crop

An historical town in the Adelaide Hills, first called Sixth Creek but later renamed Cherryville, being the first area in South Australia to cultivate cherry orchards. (See Changed Names, p. 30, Topography, p. 196.)

Christmas Hills (VIC)   Shepherds and carpenters

About 37 kilometres north-east of Melbourne is an area known as Christmas Hills, which from 1842 was occupied for grazing. Around that time a shepherd by the name of David Christmas became lost. He was eventually found and both the little hill and the locality were named after him. It's unclear whether David was found alive or dead, but given that the area was named after him, we might justifiably infer that the naming was due to the tragedy of a death and not the misadventure of being lost. The 1904 *Australian Handbook* numbered the population of the area as 250 people. It also cited a library (of 900 volumes), a state school, a mechanics' institute and an Anglican church. The 1954 census showed the population had dropped by more than 50 per cent to 115 people. In recent years, the area's proximity to Melbourne has attracted more people both as residents and visitors. (See Christmas Names, p. 49, Tasmanian Names, p. 199.)

Christmas Island (WA)   A day later — Boxing Island?

The first written record of the existence of the island was made in 1615. Captain William Mynors of the *Royal Mary* passed the island and named it on Christmas Day. The first recorded landing was in 1688 by a crew from the British buccaneer vessel, *Cygnet*, who were sent ashore by William Dampier in the vicinity of the Dales for water and timber. Although several landings were made in the next sixty-nine years, it was not until 1857 that an attempt was made by the crew of the *Amethyst* to explore the island. Their venture was limited by the inland cliffs and dense jungle. The first extensive exploration was in 1887. In 1888 Christmas Island was declared part of the British Dominion as the result of pressure from two prospective entrepreneurs. On 1 January 1958 the island, which had until then been administered as part of the Colony of Singapore, became a separate colony. On 1 October 1958, sovereignty was transferred to Australia. (See Christmas Names p. 49.)

Churchill National Park (VIC)   We shall fight
This park was named after Sir Winston Churchill. (See Dignitaries, p. 60.)

Clare (SA)   Nostalgic sheep
Named after the home county of Irishman Edward Gleeson, who established a sheep station in the Clare Valley in 1840. (See Nostalgia, p. 151.)

Clarence (WA)   Royal mention
A townsite named after Prince William, the Duke of Clarence and Earl of Munster. (See Royalty, p. 175.)

Cliftons Morass (VIC)   Close call
Named by Angus McMillan in the 1840s after his favourite horse Clifton was nearly lost in the bog. (See Horses, p. 95.)

Coburg (VIC)   Royal visit
In 1869 this area of Victoria was visited by Prince Alfred, the Duke of Saxe-Coburg. The name 'Coburg' was awarded in honour of the visit. (See Royalty, p. 175.)

Come by Chance (NSW)   You never know your luck
This strangely named place sits at the junction of two creeks.

By the time William Colless arrived in the area in 1862, there were already a number of cattle runs in the district and he thought it unlikely that he would stumble upon any unsettled land. But he did, acquiring the last available plot, which he named 'Come by Chance'. Banjo Paterson was intrigued by the name and referred to it in one of his bush ballads. (See Literary Names, p. 123.)

Como (NSW)   Real estate bait

This serene and leafy Sydney suburb, almost completely surrounded by water, was named by a local developer, James Murphy. A belief existed that he named it after Como in Italy, since it was believed to be similar. This rather romantic view has been overturned more recently — evidence has emerged that suggests the naming was more entrepreneurial, chosen more 'as a means of promoting the sale of land to those who found the mystique of foreign places difficult to resist' (Stilgoe 2004). (See Mistakes and Apocrypha, p. 139.)

Constitution Hill (TAS)   No pain, no gain

A hill that allegedly derived its name because of a remark to the effect, 'You need a damn good constitution to get to the top of that hill'.

Coober Pedy (SA)   A hole for all seasons

Allegedly derived from local Aboriginal words meaning 'white fellow's hole in the ground', and describing what the local Aboriginal people regarded as peculiar activities — both mining and living underground — by early opal seekers. The belief was that the dugouts were made to enable the prospectors to escape the heat, though they were also protection against the cold and wind at night. (See Aboriginal Names, p. 11.)

Cooktown (QLD)   Tribute to Cook

Named after Captain James Cook who beached his ship, the *Endeavour,* here. (See Dignitaries, p. 60.)

Coolangatta (QLD)   Remembering a wreck

Named after a ship, the *Coolangatta*, which was wrecked on the coast in the 1840s. It is said that the word was an anglicised Aboriginal word meaning 'beautiful place'.

Coolgardie (WA)   Safe as fridges

The name of this once-prosperous mining town on the West Australian goldfields was derived from an Aboriginal name spelt variously as 'Koolgoor-biddie', 'Coolcaby', 'Goolgardie' and 'Cookardie'. The name referred to the local mulga vegetation and waterhole. Other than gold, the town's main claim to fame was the 'Coolgardie Safe', a cooling device invented in the late 1890s to preserve perishable foods from the heat of the outback.

Coolum Beach (QLD)   Distinctive mountain

Derived from the Gabi-gabi language, 'gulum' or 'kulum', meaning 'blunt' or 'headless', referring to the shape of Mount Coolum, which has no peak. According to Aboriginal legend, Ninderry knocked off Coolum's head and it fell into the ocean where it became Mudjimba or Old Woman Island. Other meanings have also been suggested, such as 'bear', 'fat snake' and 'death adder'. (See Aboriginal Names, p. 11.)

Copernicus (VIC)   Sunnyside up

In Melbourne, two different streets are named after Polish astronomer Nicolaus Copernicus. (See Polish Names, p. 168.)

Corinna (TAS)   Look out for the tiger

Corinna is taken from the Aboriginal word for the animal known as the Tasmanian Tiger, which was once found there in abundance. The Tasmanian Tiger was such a menace to local livestock that a bounty was offered for each one killed. The animal has not been spotted for almost 70 years and is now thought to be extinct.

Cracow (QLD)   Memory rules

The town of Cracow was settled in the 1850s and named in

honour of the Polish city, which had made a brave stand for independence in 1846. The wife of one of the owners of the holdings was from Silesia in Poland, and it was her influence that led to the naming of their pastoral runs — Cracow, Silesia and Dresden. (See Polish Names, p. 168.)

Cradle Mountain (TAS)   In the eye of the beholder
So named because of a fancied resemblance to a miner's cradle.

Craven (NSW)   Careful what you wish for
Allegedly named after a shepherd known as 'Old Craven Jack' because of his ceaseless craving for a better life in a different place. The area was first known as 'Craven Flat'.

Crib Point (VIC)   Home is where the heart is
The brothers Hann were early pioneers on the Mornington Peninsula, who had their hut, or 'crib', on the point.

Crows Nest (QLD)   Home of crows
This place name is an example of the confusion that grows up around popular etymology. A popular belief is that the name comes from an Aboriginal resident who lived in a hollow tree, which apparently still stands in the town. However, there is some evidence that the legend of Jimmy Crow was invented in order to put the name on the map for tourist purposes. More recently, it would seem that the local Aboriginal name for the area was 'Tookoogandan-nah', which means 'home of crows', suggesting in itself that Jimmy Crow would have been named after the area, not the other way around (Turvey 2001).

Cubba Cubba (NSW)
A creek at Taree. (See Double Names, p. 101.)

Curie (VIC)   Polonium
Named after the famous Polish-born scientist Marie Curie (nee Sklodowska) who discovered polonium, which was named after

her native land of Poland, and radium in 1898. (See Polish Names, p. 168.)

Curl Curl (NSW)   No curls here

Situated on Sydney's northern beaches, this suburb draws its name from a local word, 'curial curial', meaning 'river of life'. (See Aboriginal Names, p. 11, Double Names, p. 101.)

Currie (TAS)   No hot food here

Located on Tasmania's King Island, the town takes its name from Captain Archibald Currie, who salvaged the sunken wreck of the *Netherby* in the late 1800s.

Currumbin (QLD)   Choice of three

Currumbin is a good example of how poorly kept were the records, where they even existed, of local indigenous languages. Three possible meanings for the Aboriginal word 'currumbin' have been put forward. One is 'high up' or 'place where high trees grow'. Another is derived from 'kurrohmin', meaning 'kangaroo'. The third is 'quicksand'. Apparently, in the old days of travel along the coast, there was a ford across the creek at Currumbin, which could be negotiated at low tide but had to be taken carefully owing to the quicksand that was prevalent there at the time.

Cygnet (TAS)   Swan song

Located on the Huon River, Cygnet was originally named 'Port des Cygnes' by the French Admiral D'Entrecasteaux, who was moved by the large number of black swans living there. Over time the name of the town evolved into the present one, its original meaning now lost.

Cynthia Bay (TAS)   Luna magic

This bay was named after the Greek mythological goddess of the moon. (See Tasmanian Names, p. 199.)

CHRISTMAS NAMES

Over one hundred place names around Australia, including some in every state and territory, have a Christmas theme. Below is a non-exhaustive sampling.

Place name	State/territory
Angel Creek	NSW
Angel Gully	SA
Angel Island	WA
Angels Beach	NSW
Bell	QLD
Bells Beach	VIC
Carol Creek	QLD
Celebration Bore, Celebration Dam, Celebration Mine, Celebration Park	WA
Celebration Reef	QLD
Christmas Bay, Christmas Cove	TAS
Christmas Bore	NT
Christmas Box Creek, Christmas Bush Creek, Christmas Day Creek	NSW
Christmas Creek	NT, QLD, SA, TAS
Christmas Creek, Christmas Gift, Christmas Gift Mine, Christmas Hill	WA
Christmas Day Lagoon	QLD
Christmas Hills	TAS, VIC
Christmas Island	WA
Christmas Ridge	VIC
Christmas, Christmas Cove	SA
Comet, Comet Ledge	QLD
Comet Bay	WA
Comet Creek	TAS

Christmas Names

Place name	State/territory
Comet Range	WA
Decoration Cave	WA
Gift Dam	SA
Golden Gift Mine	WA
Holly Creek	QLD
Holly Hill	WA
Holly Spring	NT
Jolly Beach, Jolly Creek	SA
Jolly Creek	QLD
Jolly Creek	NSW
Lake Surprise	NT, SA, TAS, VIC, WA
Mistletoe	QLD
Mistletoe Bore, Mistletoe Dam, Mistletoe Island, Mistletoe Well	WA
Mistletoe Creek	TAS
Mount Holly	QLD
Mount Surprise	QLD
Noel, Noel Creek, Noel Island	QLD
Noel Dam	NT
North Pole, North Pole Creek	WA
North Pole Swamp	NSW
Reindeer Lagoon, Reindeer Rock	QLD
Rudolph Gap	VIC
St Nicholas Inlet	NT
Silver Star Creek	VIC
Star	QLD
Surprise Creek	NSW, NT, QLD, TAS, VIC, WA
Xmas Dam	SA

D

Daintree (QLD)   **Friendship**

The name 'Daintree' was given to the town, river and national park by the explorer George Dalrymple, after a friend of his, Richard Daintree, in 1873. Daintree was an English geologist and photographer who had spent time in Australia, discovered gold in various places and returned to England because of ill health.

Daisy Hill (QLD)   **Floral tribute**

There are two versions of the origins of this place name: it may have been named after a woman called Daisy who ran a brothel in the area; or to honour the profusion of wild daisies that grow in the locality.

Damascus Gate (TAS)   **Main entrance**

This is the name of a pass. Damascus Gate is the main gate into the old city of Jerusalem. (See Tasmanian Names, p. 199.)

Dandaloo (NSW)   **French influence**

Presumed to have been named after a town in France. (See Nostalgia, p. 151.)

Darwin (NT)   Famous voyage

Named after the British naturalist Charles Darwin who had
sailed on a previous journey of the *Beagle* with Captain John
Clements Wickham, who arrived in the harbour in 1839. (See
Dignitaries, p. 60.)

Day Dawn (WA)   Sunrise

In the last decade of the nineteenth century, the West Australian
gold township of Day Dawn was named by a local gold prospector
after the time of day that he pegged his claim. (See Special
Days, p. 186.)

Dayboro (QLD)   Horsy origin

Previously called Terror's Creek, allegedly after a prized Arab
stallion whose name was actually 'Terah' and was said to instil
terror in the locals. The name was later changed to Hamilton
after a local farmer and then again to Dayboro, in 1919, after
William Henry Day, a police magistrate in Brisbane. (See
Changed Names, p. 30, Horses, p. 95.)

Dead Heart of Australia (SA)   Non-mincing words

An arid area in the vicinity of Lake Eyre, Curdimurka and the
Simpson Desert, named by the geologist John Simpson in 1901.
(See Topography, p. 196.)

Dead Man Crossing (QLD)   Risky business

This ford was named as a result of being the site of five drownings.
The first was that of a young man who was swept off his feet
while his mother looked on helplessly. He was buried on an
adjacent sand hill over which, according to a local legend, a
light appears to flicker at night. (See Pessimistic Names,
p. 165.)

Dead Secret (NSW)   You can't take it with you

Allegedly named because of a gold prospector in Dubbo
who, having dug up some nuggets of exceptional size, refused
to reveal the location of his find. He was followed and then

found dead. His gold was never found and its whereabouts remained a 'dead secret'.

Death Rock (SA)   Rocky point of exit

This feature of the landscape has been described as 'an interesting lump by a waterhole'. The local indigenous name for it is 'kanyaka', meaning 'a piece of rock'. The early white settlers noticed that sick and dying Aboriginal people would go there to die and they named it accordingly. (See Pessimistic Names, p. 165.)

Deception Bay (QLD)   Seeing isn't believing

This bay takes its name from Deception River, being the name given to Pine River when John Finnegan mistakenly took John Oxley up it in the belief that it was the big river that later became the Brisbane River. (See Pessimistic Names, p. 165.)

Dee Why (NSW)   Mysterious letters

The northern suburb of Sydney that is today known as Dee Why was named by the surveyor James Meehan in 1815. That much is known. But why he chose the name and what it means are questions that have remained a mystery. At that time, Meehan was surveying several 'promised land' grants along the northern beaches of Sydney. On the day in question, he wrote in his Survey Book 99, 'Wednesday 27 September, 1815, Dy beach —50 acres (20 hectares)' and then the name 'Thomas Bruin', in whose name the land grant was promised. In subsequent notes, he referred to 'Dy Bay' and 'Dy Lagoon'. He later amended the 'Dy' to 'D Y', as if to clarify the pronunciation, but at no time did he indicate what he meant by the letters. With time the 'D' and 'Y' became 'Deewhy' and later 'Dee Why'. There is, however, no shortage of speculation and suggestions. Some (not all!) of these, both plausible and fantastic, are listed below, the order having no significance in terms of probability.

- Meehan's note 'Dy beach' stands for 'dirty beach'.
- The name originated when a ship under the command of

Captain De Vegas was lost off the South American coast, blown to Australia, and wrecked at the place we now know as 'Dee Why'. According to the legend, the captain was supposed to have carved his initials into the rock. He managed the 'D' but in carving the 'V' his hand slipped, and it turned into a 'Y'. Another version of the wrecked ship notion is that the Spanish ship *Donna Ysabel* arrived off the coast of Australia, intending to go to South America. The captain carved the name into the rocks, while his men went off seeking gold.

- From a certain vantage point (which has remained unspecified) the beach and lagoon in the area resembled the letters 'D' and 'Y'.

- The lagoon was inhabited by a bird that made the sound 'dee wee', which early settlers anglicised into 'Dee Why'. One version claims the 'Dy' in Meehan's notes was his attempt to capture the sound of the bird.

- The name is an adaptation or corruption of an Aboriginal word of unknown origin, perhaps an Aboriginal word for 'stingray', with which the lagoon was plagued in the early days.

- Just as 'Woy Woy' is a corruption of 'Wy Wy', an Aboriginal name for that area, meaning 'big lagoon', Meehan may have written 'Dy' and meant 'double Y'.

- The word is an Aboriginal word for 'wood' — the idea here is that the area was known for its resource of wood for the new settlers.

- 'Dy' may have been a surveyor's reference of the time, indicating an unfinished line, but modern surveyors cast doubt on this, claiming the term was not used in Meehan's time.

- The name honours the Irish name 'Deey', pronounced Dee Why, a not uncommon family name in Dublin. It was commonplace to name places after family and place names from home. Like so many of the convicts transported to Australia, Meehan was Irish, having been transported to the colony in 1800 because of his participation in the 1798 rebellion.

- 'Dy' comes from Meehan's native Gaelic language — sometimes in Irish writings the letters D V appear (meaning Deo Volentre, or God Willing) but nothing is known about 'Dy'.

- The 'Dy' stands for 'Deputy': Meehan in fact was Deputy Surveyor-General to Governor Macquarie, who in his own journal used the abbreviation 'Dy' to describe Meehan's position.
- The 'Dy' stands for 'D'Arcy' referring to D'Arcy Wentworth, a well-known figure at the time, to whom Bruin had sold his land even before it had been registered by Meehan. Such abbreviations of first names were common in documents of the time, for example, 'Hy' for 'Henry' or 'Harry', 'Wm' for 'William'. A version of this is that 'Dy' stood for 'Deey', which was the maiden name of Wentworth's daughter's mother-in-law. And another version says the 'dy' stands for the Greek word 'dyspros', meaning 'difficulty of access'.

DEVILISH NAMES

An interesting aspect of place names around Australia is the number of Christmas associations (see Christmas Names, p. 49). What is less known is the influence of the devil on place naming. In NSW alone, there are nineteen geographic locations that feature 'hell hole' in their place name.

The following list shows some of the devil's influence in Victoria.

Devils Bend Reservoir
Hellhole Creek
The Devils Basin
The Devils Elbow
The Devils Hole
The Devils Kitchen

In the words of Chris Richards, 'What these places seem to have in common is a remote location, rugged landscape, and an element of danger' (Richards, personal correspondence). The purpose of the name at the time of naming would seem to be to provide a signal to avoid such places, or visit them at one's peril.

Denial Bay (SA)   A role for St Peter

The first European settlement in the Ceduna area occurred in the 1840s on the shores of Denial Bay, an area first explored by Matthew Flinders. He named the bay both because it denied entry into a larger body of water and because the name was an oblique allusion to the island of St Peter off the coast, St Peter having denied Christ three times. (See Pessimistic Names, p. 165.)

D'Entrecasteaux Channel (TAS)   French waterway

French Explorer Bruni D'Entrecasteaux named this sheltered waterway after himself in 1792. In the early days this channel was favoured by whalers and formed a bustling shipping way between the capital city Hobart and a number of towns that sprang up along its shores. (See Exploration Names, p. 66.)

Derry Derry (QLD)

A creek south of Mount Isa. (See Double Names, p. 101.)

Devils Marbles (NT)

So named on account of these granite boulders sized from 20 centimetres to 6 metres in diameter. (See Topography, p. 196.)

Devitt Hill (NT)   Short-wave hazards

In 1960, a surveyor working in the Alice Springs (NT) area heard the results of the 1960 Rome Olympics on his short-wave radio. Australia's top three swimmers had done extremely well. In his enthusiasm, the surveyor named some of the features of the land he was surveying after the names of the athletes who had done so well — Devitt Hill after John Devitt, Frazer Hill after Dawn Fraser, and Tylers Pass after David Theile. But the radio reception was poor. The surveyor did not see the names written down and did not expect that the names as given would in the end become official. But they did, and once the names were entered on the maps, it was too late, in the case of Frazer Hill and Tylers Pass, to correct the spelling. And that is how they remain.

Dig Tree (QLD)   A tragedy of errors

This is the name given to a landmark coolabah tree in south-western Queensland on the South Australian border, where 'one of the saddest stories in the history of Australian inland exploration' took place. Explorers Burke and Wills left a party of men at a depot near the tree as they themselves, and their party of men, set out to push north towards the Gulf of Carpentaria. Their return trip was delayed by many obstacles, the trek becoming increasingly desperate as their supplies and time ran out. They made it back, but just hours after it had been abandoned by the original group. Burke recovered a cache of food left buried at the base of the tree, where William Brahe, the leader of the group, had carved 'DIG'. Burke then left a letter telling of his decision to head south-west. But he smoothed the ground over and when the worried Brahe returned two weeks later, he assumed from the undisturbed appearance of the ground near the tree that they had never returned. Meanwhile, Burke's party floundered westward and most ended up starving to death 'in a land which provided its Aboriginal inhabitants with abundant food' (*Readers Digest Illustrated Guide to Australian Places*, 2003).

Dimboola (VIC)   Faraway figs

The town of Dimboola developed from a crude bush village called 'Nine Creeks', which was begun around 1859 to serve the needs of local squatters. The name is believed to be connected to the fact that, after a flood, the river receded, leaving nine creeks. Within a decade, the place was surveyed and the town of Dimboola gazetted. The name 'Dimboola' calls on the surveyor's experience of travelling in Sri Lanka. It means 'land of figs', appropriate because many of the fruit trees of the area were figs. The town was made famous by the play *Dimboola* by Jack Hibberd (1969). (See Literary Names, p. 123.)

Dimbulah (QLD)
A Muluridji Aborignal word for 'long waterhole'. (See Aboriginal Names, p. 11.)

Dinner Plain (VIC)   Anyone hungry?
Dinner Plain is a small ski village situated in the Great Dividing Range, 12 kilometres south-east of Mount Hotham. All its buildings are designed in an Australian alpine style based on early cattlemen's huts. The village was constructed in the late 1980s as a dormitory for Mount Hotham. It takes its name from the plain where, last century, the coach from Bright to Omeo used to stop for dinner.

Dinosaur Point (SA)   Jurassic paws
Fossilised footsteps of a dinosaur have been found at the foot of the cliffs. (See Topography, p. 196.)

Doctors Creek (QLD)   Bad luck story
Named after a horse that had been bought from a horse doctor and thus called 'Doctor'. The horse got stuck in the mud and died. (See Horses, p. 95.)

Dog on the Tuckerbox (NSW)
Named after the anonymous poem 'Bullocky Bill', which first told the tale of the dog that disgraced himself in the tucker box 'five miles from Gundagai'. This was echoed in the poem 'Nine Miles from Gundagai', which later became part of Australian folk legend. (See Literary Names, p. 123.)

Doganabuganaram Hill (NSW)   Bed sharing
Many events are captured in the name of a place. There's the story of the surveyor who was exploring the Mendooran area and when it was time to camp for the night, he found he had to share his camp with a dog and a bug and a ram. The name of the hill where he camped is now called Doganabuganaram Hill.

Donnybrook (WA)   Golden don
Located 206 kilometres south of Perth, Donnybrook was the

centre of a short but profitable gold rush when in 1897 gold was discovered there. Donnybrook was named after a suburb in Dublin, Ireland, from where its first settlers originated.

Doo Town (TAS)   The power of positive thinking
A town in Tasmania where every house has a name such as 'Can Doo' or 'It'll Doo' or 'Howdya Doo'. The first house to set the trend was 'Doo Little'. Others are 'Doo Us', 'Doo Me', 'Doo Nix', 'Wee Doo', 'Xanadu', 'Rum Doo', 'Do Nothing', 'Doo More', 'Do F@#% All', 'Didgeri-Doo', 'Doo Come In', 'Doodle Doo', 'Kakka-Doo', 'Wattle-I-Doo'. (See Tasmanian Names, p. 199.)

Dorrigo (NSW)   A Spanish hero in the stringy bark?
The name of a town in northern NSW, Dorrigo is an example of a common occurrence in place-naming research in which two purported origins — one local, Aboriginal, the other European — come to light and both seem plausible. One view about Dorrigo is that the name comes from a General Don Dorrigo, who was a Spanish military hero. However, a current resident of Dorrigo refutes this, saying that no such military hero existed, a fact confirmed by the Spanish Military Academy in Madrid. The alternative theory about the name of Dorrigo says that it is a word from the local Gumbainggir people that means 'stringy bark' or 'edge of the world'. (See Mistakes and Apocrypha, p. 139.)

Dover (TAS)   French influence
Dover was earlier called Port Esperance, after one of the ships in Bruni D'Entrecasteaux's 1792 expedition. It was later renamed Dover after the English seaport of the same name. (See Changed Names, p. 30, Nostalgia, p. 151.)

Dubbo (NSW)   Warm head or red earth
Dubbo was first reported on by the explorer John Oxley during expeditions in 1817–18. The name, some believe, is a corruption of the local native word 'tubbo', meaning a head covering made

of possum fur. Others say it comes from an Aboriginal word for 'red earth'.

Dundee Beach (NT)   Crocodiles all around

Like the localities of Dundee Downs and Dundee Forest, Dundee Beach is believed to be named after the 1988 Australian film, *Crocodile Dundee.*

DIGNITARIES

The early settlers often named the places they found in tribute to current or deceased dignitaries, especially those who held public office, were members of the British aristocracy, or were considered to have made important contributions to society.

Place name	State/ territory	Dignitary
Batchelor	NT	A South Australian and federal politician, Egerton Batchelor.
Bathurst	NSW	Earl Bathurst, British Secretary of State for the Colonies.
Broome	WA	The Governor of Western Australia, Frederick N Broome.
Cape Jervis	SA	The family name of the Earl of St Vincent, a Lord Commissioner of the Admiralty.
Churchill National Park	VIC	Sir Winston Churchill.
Cooktown	QLD	Captain James Cook.
Darwin	NT	The British naturalist Charles Darwin.
Fremantle	WA	Captain Charles Fremantle (1800–69).
Gore Hill	NSW	Provost Marshall William Gore.
Hobart	TAS	Robert Hobart, Secretary of State for War and the Colonies.

Place name	State/territory	Dignitary
Macquarie	NSW	Lachlan Macquarie, Governor of NSW.
Melbourne	VIC	Lord Melbourne, the British Prime Minister of the time.
Murray River	NSW, SA, VIC	The English statesman, Sir George Murray.
Pitt Town	NSW	The famous English politician, William Pitt.
Port Arthur	TAS	Governor George Arthur.
Sydney	NSW	Named after the British Home Secretary, Thomas Townshend, Lord Sydney (later, Viscount Sydney). The local Eora name is 'Warrane'.
Wilberforce	NSW	William Wilberforce, eighteenth-century anti-slavery campaigner.

Earhardt (NT)
A name linked to aviation

The undeveloped area on the western side of the upper reaches of the Middle Arm of Darwin Harbour takes its name from Amelia Earhardt, who was born in Kansas in 1898. In 1932 she flew a Lockheed Vega from Newfoundland to Ireland, landing at Donegal. Her visit to Darwin in the pre-war days of early aviation exploits ended when she mysteriously became lost north of Lae in New Guinea on 3 July 1937. She was attempting to fly to Howland Island and Hawaii when she disappeared. Perhaps befitting its name and the connection to aviation history, the site of Earhardt is a recommended area for a second airport in Darwin's long-term strategy plan.

Eden (NSW)
A kind of paradise

The town of Eden is a very beautiful spot in the far southern corner of NSW, very close to the border with Victoria. Originally settled by whalers, the early history of the bay is closely tied to the whaling industry. Today, Eden is a fishing port and also a popular holiday resort town, as yet relatively undeveloped. This idyllic coastal town is bounded to the north and south by national park and by woodland to the west.

The area of Eden is thought to have been inhabited by the Thawa Aborigines prior to white settlement. George Bass noted Twofold Bay in December 1797 as he travelled south down the NSW coast. On his return in early 1798, he entered the bay that he called Snug Cove because of the security it offered to vessels. The following year, Bass set out again with Matthew Flinders and it was on this trip that they made contact with local Aborigines. Flinders recorded the meeting in his diary. He offered them some biscuits and received some fat (probably whale fat) in return. After tasting it, Flinders wrote that while 'watching an opportunity to spit it out when he should not be looking, I perceived him doing precisely the same thing with our biscuit'.

Although it's tempting to think that Eden, beautiful as it is, was named after the Bible's Garden of Eden, in fact it was named after the British Secretary for the Colonies, Baron Auckland, whose family name was Eden.

Eglinton (WA)   Wrecked on rocks
This suburb of Perth was approved in 1973. It was named after the barque *Eglinton*, which in 1852 was wrecked on rocks, now called Eglinton Rocks, located off the coast adjacent to the suburb. (See Ship Names, p. 183.)

Eidsvold (QLD)   Nordic influence
Named by a Scottish family, the Archers, who had moved to Norway in the 1820s and from there to Australia, where they named their run after the Norwegian village famous for being the place where the Norwegian constitution was passed into law. (See Nostalgia, p. 151.)

Ellangowan (NSW)   The uncle is welcome
This village on the NSW coast bears an Aboriginal name. Originally named Gowan Gowan from Bundjalung 'gawang', meaning maternal uncle, the name perhaps refers to a ceremony in which uncles were involved.

Elliston (SA)   www

Originally known as Ellie's Town, Elliston was named for a governess Ellen Liston who lived on a local station. It stands on the shores of Waterloo Bay, with a highly dangerous entry owing to the reefs lying between the two headlands — Wellington and Wellesley Points. The naming has historical significance, as Arthur Wellesley was the Duke of Wellington who defeated Napoleon at the Battle of Waterloo.

Elong Elong (NSW)

A rail siding east of Dubbo. (See Double Names, p. 101.)

Elrington (NSW)   More than one Elrington

In 1840 this area was granted to one Clement Elrington and his memory lives on in the name of the locality. It is not to be confused with Majors Creek, which was named after another Elrington, Major William Sandys Elrington, with the name being formally awarded in 1928.

Emerald (VIC)   A golden death

In the 1850s, a brief gold rush in this area brought in the prospectors, one of whom was called Jack Emerald who ended up murdered, giving his name to a local creek and later to the town that developed in the 1880s.

Emu Plains (NSW)   When is an emu not an emu?

So named due to an abundance of emus in the area. The name 'emu' is not an Aboriginal word, as is often mistakenly assumed. It seems to have been derived from an Arabic word for 'large bird' and subsequently adopted by Portuguese explorers, who used it to refer to cassowaries in Indonesia. Later explorers used the word for the bird now known as the emu.

Encounter Bay (SA)   A faraway conflict

This name celebrates the encounter between explorers Matthew Flinders and Nicolas Baudin, which was amicable despite the fact that England and France were at war.

Enngonia (NSW)   Bush ballads

This township north of Burke is associated with a number of bush balladeers in late nineteenth-century outback Australia such as Will Ogilvie and Henry Lawson. (See Literary Names, p. 123.)

Eora Beach (NSW)   Local forebears

The term is derived from the word 'ora', which probably means 'country' or 'place'. Some use 'Eora' to refer to the Aboriginal coastal tribes living between Port Jackson and Botany Bay.

Ephraims Gate (TAS)   Fruit of Jacob's loins

This is the name of a pass. Ephraim's Gate is the northern gate into the old city of Jerusalem — Ephraim was the younger son of Jacob. (See Tasmanian Names, p. 199.)

Ettamogah (NSW)   Here's to us

Popularly considered to be derived from a local Aboriginal word for 'let's have a drink', which may or may not be related to the vineyards in the area. (See Aboriginal Names, p. 11.)

Eurelia (SA)   Depends on how you say it

This name is believed to be derived from an Aboriginal word. Legend has it that a traveller arriving at a station heard two porters shouting the name. One said, 'You're a liar' and the other one said, 'You really are'. The latter is the correct pronunciation.

Eurunderee (NSW)   A poet's school

Poet Henry Lawson was schooled in Eurunderee, which features in his poem 'The Old Bark School'. (See Literary Names, p. 123.)

Eversons Creek (NSW)   From canes to creeks

Named after a local settler, James Everson who was born at Chatsworth Island on the Clarence River in 1881. He came to the Richmond area in 1900 and subsequently purchased a cane farm on this spot, where he lived until his death in 1963.

Ewingsdale (NSW)   A name in exchange for a train

Just outside Byron Bay, this village was named after a politician, Sir Thomas Thomson Ewing (1856–1920), a former surveyor in the area. Sir Thomas held the portfolios of Postmaster-General, Home Affairs and Defence and is best remembered for the railway he had built from Lismore to Murwillumbah.

EXPLORATION NAMES

Like the colonists in the American West, early Europeans were eager to explore the vast country of Australia. Sometimes this was driven by economic motives, with explorers being contracted on behalf of other groups or interests. Sometimes, it was more the spirit of adventure that made people want to know what was over the next hill. So it is no surprise, given the early colonial history of Australia, that many place names around the country are named after explorers.

Often the name was given by the explorer who 'found' the place. Other times it was given by a subsequent explorer, to mark the contribution of the one who was there before. Frequently, the name was given for a member of the team who had died in the effort; other times it was given later in honour of an explorer important to the area.

Sometimes the motive was more evidently economic, such as in cases where explorers named new places after their patrons or after those they wished would fund them in further explorations. This was expected within the complicated patronage system of the time. After all, immortality bestowed in a place name was not likely to go unnoticed and from such quarters might come funding for the next adventure.

The following is evidence of the impact of exploration on place names in Australia.

Place name	State/territory	Explorers
Bass Strait	TAS	Matthew Flinders honoured his co-explorer George Bass.
Bells Mountain	NSW	Named after the explorer Lieutenant Archibald Bell.
Blaxland	NSW	Named after explorer Gregory Blaxland.
Buccaneer Archipelago	WA	Captain Phillip Parker King honoured William Dampier, a swashbuckling buccaneer. The bay that fronts the islands was called Cygnet Bay after Dampier's vessel.
Burketown	QLD	Named after the explorer Robert O'Hara Burke.
D'Entrecasteaux Channel	TAS	Named by French explorer Bruni D'Entrecasteaux after himself.
Flinders Ranges	SA	Named after explorer Matthew Flinders.
King Sound	WA	Named after the explorer Phillip Parker King.
Leichhardt	NSW	Named after Ludwig Leichhardt, a German explorer, scientist and geologist.
Mount Oxley	NSW	Explorer Charles Sturt honoured explorer John Oxley.
Raymond Terrace	NSW	Named after Midshipman Raymond, who remarked on the 'terraced' appearance of the trees up the Hunter River.
Strzelecki Track	SA	Named in honour of Polish-born explorer Paul Edmund de Strzelecki.
Sturt Stony Desert	SA	Named after the explorer Charles Sturt.

Fairmile Cove (NSW)   Ship builders

This cove in the Parramatta River was named after the 'Fairmile' class of naval ship, twenty of which were constructed in this bay during the later stages of World War II. These vessels played a major role in the outcome of the war. (See Measured Names, p. 130, War Names, p. 218.)

Fannie Bay (NT)   Opera in exile

This suburb of Darwin was named in 1868, after Fanny Carandini, a popular opera singer of the time. She was the daughter of an exiled Italian count, who went to Tasmania in the 1840s where he married a noted opera singer, Maria Burgess. Madame Carandini and her daughters, Fanny, Rosina and Lizzie, formed a famous singing group, travelling widely in Australia and overseas.

Farmers Creek (NSW)   Bad name for a horse

Once upon a time there was a horse called 'Farmer'. It was owned by Major Thomas Mitchell, but it drowned in the Murrumbidgee River. Mitchell subsequently acquired another horse, which he also called 'Farmer'. The second 'Farmer' fell into a creek and broke its neck near Lithgow. The creek was later named Farmer's Creek. Apparently, Mitchell later observed that 'Farmer' was 'an unfortunate appellation for a surveyor's horse' (Hungerford & Donald 1982).

Farrell Flat (SA)   Choose your Farrell
A small settlement once had the official name of Hanson but was called Farrell's Flat by the locals. The name was finally changed in 1940, at which time it lost its possessive form. The origins of the name remain a mystery. One story says it was named after James Farrell, a shepherd who worked on an early squatter's sheep run. Another has it that it was named after a famous South Australian chaplain, also called James Farrell, whose buggy once became bogged in this area.

Fennells Bay (NSW)   Oxford pioneer
This pretty bay was named after a pioneer named Richard Fennell, a graduate of Oxford who came to Newcastle in 1847.

Fig Tree Pocket (QLD)   Figs of yore
A suburb of Brisbane in a 'river pocket' where once fig trees grew. (See Topography, p. 196.)

Figure of Eight Creek (TAS)   Quirky
A creek that flows into the Mersey River near Devonport and, contradicting its name, follows an orderly course. (See Tasmanian Names, p. 199.)

Fingal (TAS)
Named after an Irish town of the same name. (See Nostalgia, p. 151.)

Fingal Bay (NSW)   Mistaken entry
The former name of Fingal Bay was False Bay, so named because the mariners who were exploring the area came to grief mistaking it for the entrance to Port Stephens. (See Pessimistic Names, p. 165.)

Fishers Ghost Creek (NSW)   Trust your ghost

A local resident of the town, a John Farley, reputedly saw a ghost at Campbelltown in 1826, which he recognised as Fred Fisher. No one believed him, in part because Fisher had left the district some time before. Farley insisted that Fisher had been pointing at the creek, and it was in the creek that police eventually found Fisher's body. The story has gone into local lore.

Flat Rock Creek (NSW)   Ask the locals

A spring forms the headwaters for this watercourse. The spring rises in an area that contains a large, flat rock and consequently is known to the locals as 'Flat Rock'.

Fleming Gully (NSW)   For better or worse

The creek flows through land that was originally granted to Patrick Fleming last century. Later, a descendant, James Fleming, was drowned in a nearby well.

Flinders Ranges (SA)   Spotted from sea

Named after Matthew Flinders, the first white man to see the mountain range, during his circumnavigation of Australia between 1801 and 1803. It was Flinders who suggested the name 'Australia', which was adopted in 1824. (See Exploration Names, p. 66.)

Florence Head (NSW)   Honour thyself

Named after Surveyor Florence who carried out a survey in 1828 from Jervis Bay to Mount Dromedary.

Fly Creek (NT)   No flies on him

This locality takes its name from Fly Creek, which was applied by William Harvey when surveying sections of the Hundred of Cavenagh. (The word 'Hundred' is used in the Top End of the Northern Territory and South Australia. It originates in the English local government feudal system of land subdivision. It is believed that a 'Hundred' was the land occupied by a group of people who provided one hundred warriors for the national army.) George Goyder was the South Australian surveyor who was responsible for carrying out the first freehold surveys in this area of the Northern Territory. As there were no members of his party with the name of 'Fly', it is assumed that Harvey was worried by flies in the area.

Folly Point (NSW)   If at first you don't succeed
Reportedly named after a builder called Folly, who repeatedly built a house on the point using salt water in the mortar. The house collapsed every time.

Forster (NSW)   Pay rise needed
The headland south of Forster was sighted and named 'Cape Hawke' after Baron Hawke, a British naval officer, by Captain James Cook. The entry was made in the ship's log of 11 May 1770. Forster was named in 1870 after William Forster, Secretary for Lands. That year the first school was built, and its first teacher, a graduate of Cambridge University, taught for a salary of threepence a week or a donation of meat and potatoes.

Fort Denison (NSW)   Pinchgut
When European settlement began in Sydney, 'Pinchgut Island', known by Aborigines as 'Matteweye', was a jagged, rocky outcrop in the harbour, used as a place of solitary confinement for difficult convicts by the early colonial governors. In 1855, it was razed to sea level and then became part of Sydney's defences. The gun batteries, barracks and tower were built by the chief engineer of public works, Colonel George Barney. It was he who suggested that the fort be named after the Governor, Sir William Denison. (See Dual Names, p. 107.)

Fortitude Valley (QLD)   Strength in adversity
This suburb of Brisbane was named after the immigrant ship *Fortitude* that brought prospective migrants to Moreton Bay in 1848. The new arrivals first lived in this locality. They mistakenly believed that on arrival they would be given land. Instead, they were allowed to form a shantytown. They named the area after

the vessel that brought them, and probably also out of the test of character the experience required of them. (See Pessimistic Names, p. 165.)

Fotheringham Gully (NSW)   Original settlers

This name commemorates the original inhabitants in the area, who lived there over 100 years ago and the gully has been known as Fotheringham Gully ever since.

Franklin River (TAS)   Some walk, some are carried

This famous, mighty river in Tasmania was named after a Governor of the colony, Sir John Franklin, who arranged to have an overland track cut and surveyed from Lake St Clair to Macquarie Harbour. After its completion, in two years, the Governor and his official party completed the walk in twenty days. During this time, for parts of the journey, Lady Jane Franklin was carried on a chair-like device. (See Royalty, p. 175.)

Fremantle (WA)   Port-maker

Named after Captain Charles Fremantle (1800–69) who established the port at the mouth of the Swan River in 1829. (See Dignitaries, p. 60.)

French Island (VIC)   French sailors

Named 'Ile de Françoise' by sailors from one of the French expedition ships, *Le Naturaliste*, in April 1802. (See French Names, p. 73.)

FRENCH NAMES

It is often said, partly in jest, that Australia might have easily become a French-speaking, not an English-speaking nation (Bloomfield 2004). Although there are strong reasons to explain why the early French naval expeditions did not end in settlement, whereas the British did, the extent of French interest in and exploration of Australia is not widely known. In fact, there was sustained French interest in the Australian continent for some three hundred years, bringing French explorers into southern waters between 1503 and 1838.

Name	State/territory	Origin
Cape Adieux	SA	The point at which French explorer Nicolas Baudin completed his charting of the coast of Australia.
Cape Duquesne	VIC	This cape is presumed to be named after the French naval commander Abraham Marquis Duquesne (1610–88).
Cape Marengo	VIC	Presumably honours Napoleon's victory in the battle of Marengo.
Cape Poivre	WA	Named after Pierre Poivre, who introduced East Indian spices to France.
Cape Reamur	VIC	Named after French scientist René Réaumur.
Cape Rose	WA	Named after the young wife of Louis-Claude de Freycinet.
Cape Volney	VIC	Believed to have been named after the historian, travel writer and philosopher, Constantin Volney.
French Island	VIC	Named 'Ile de Françoise' by sailors from the French expedition ship, *Le Naturaliste.*

French Names

Name	State/ territory	Origin
Hamelin Pool	WA	Named after Nicolas Baudin's second-in-command, Emmanuel Hamelin.
Huon River	TAS	Named by French explorer Bruni D'Entrecasteaux after his captain, Huon de Kermadec.
La Perouse	NSW	Named after the Count of La Perouse, a famous navigator.
Lancelin	WA	Derived from the name of nearby Lancelin Island, honouring author P F Lancelin.
Montmorency	VIC	Named after a farm that was itself named after the French town where Jean Jacques Rousseau lived.
Peron	WA	Named after naturalist François Péron.
Sans Souci	NSW	Named after the Sans Souci Palace, which the Prussian King Friedrich the Great built.
Kermandie River	TAS	Named after Huon de Kermadec.
Venus Bay	VIC	Called 'Baie de la Venus', after the ship Venus in which George Bass sailed to the Pacific Islands.
Vivonne Bay	SA	Named after Louis Victor de Rochechouart, Duc de Mortemart et de Vivonne.

G

Gabbin (WA)　　　　Water water everywhere
This name for a townsite in the eastern agricultural area was
derived from 'gabbabin', thought to be a local Aboriginal Nyoongar
word relating to water. (See Aboriginal Names, p. 11.)

Gabo Island (VIC)　　　We don't understand
Named by Captain James Cook in 1770 evidently because
when asked the name of the locality, the Aborigines replied
'gabo', meaning 'we don't understand'. There's a belief that this
scenario repeated itself across the continent, resulting in many
places being named the equivalent of 'we don't understand' in
the local indigenous language. This, too, may be apocryphal.

Gang Gang (NSW)
A mountain 20 kilometres south-east of Kiandra. (See Double
Names, p. 101.)

Garden Island (WA)　　　From French to English
Garden Island was earlier called Buache after the French
geographer and historian Phillippe Buache. (See Changed
Names, p. 30.)

Gate of the Chain (TAS)   Biblical reminder

This pass was named after a part of the old city of Jerusalem that serves as the entrance to the Temple Mount, leading to the Dome of the Rock and the El Aksa Mosque. (See Tasmanian Names, p. 199.)

General Kleeberg Park (NSW)   Proud Poles

A park in Maitland, founded by the local Polish Association, and named after the former president of the Federal Council of Polish Associations in Australia. The first town park created by an Australian ethnic group and given to the public, it was formally handed over to the people of Maitland in 1979. (See Polish Names, p. 168.)

Gerringong (NSW)   Risky place

The popular explanation is that the word relates to the fearful exclamations uttered by the Aborigines when they first saw the sails of the *Endeavour* in 1770. An alternative view holds that the word means 'place of peril'.

Gida Gida (NT)

A hill north-west of Alice Springs. (See Double Names, p. 101.)

Ginninderra (ACT)   Twinkle twinkle

Originally the name of a creek that flows through Belconnen but now also another suburb, its name derived from an Aboriginal word meaning 'sparkling like the stars'. (See Aboriginal Names, p. 11.)

Glasshouse Mountains (QLD)   A singular elevation

The first European to see these mountains was Captain James Cook, who wrote in his journal on 17 May 1770, 'If any future navigator should be disposed to determine the question whether there is or is not a river in this place, which the wind would not permit us to do, the situation may be always found by three hills, which lie to the northward of it, in the latitude of twenty-six degrees, fifty-three minutes. These hills lie but a little way inland, and not far from each other: they are remarkable for the singular form of their elevation, which very much resembles a glass house, and for this reason I called them the Glass Houses' (www.walkabout.com.au).

Glebe (NSW)   How 'a glebe' lost its 'a'

A 'glebe' is 'a portion of land assigned to a clergyman as part of his benefice'. In 1790, acting on instructions from London, Governor Arthur Phillip ordered 162 hectares on the outskirts of Sydney Cove settlement to be set aside for the exclusive use of the Church of England, as well as the maintenance of its pastor and the colony's first chaplain, Richard Johnson. It was a thickly wooded terrain, the clearing and cultivation of which required a great deal of work. As Johnson could only obtain the services of three convicts to help him, the glebe actually failed to contribute to the church's income. Thirty-eight years later, more than half the land was sold to raise funds for the clergy, who by then were quite impoverished. At first it was bought by wealthy merchants and professionals who built many stately mansions. In the mid-nineteenth century, some land and estates were subdivided to accommodate the influx of working-class families and the waves of immigrants arriving from Britain. A sea of terraces and cottages grew up. What started out as 'a glebe' later lost its 'a' and became 'Glebe'.

Glendon (NSW)   Memories of home

Named by Robert and Helena Scott after their home in Scotland. (See Nostalgia, p. 151.)

Glenelg (SA)   Forwards and backwards

Originally known as Holdfast Bay, this beachside suburb of Adelaide was renamed in 1837 after the Secretary of State for the Colonies, Lord Glenelg. The name is also a palindrome — but not the longest palindromic place name in Australia. That dubious honour goes to Paraparap near Geelong in Victoria.

Gnowangerup (WA)   The fate of 'up'

This centre of a major sheep-producing area derives its name from an Aboriginal word meaning 'the place where the mallee hen made her nest'. Interestingly enough, the town once wished to change the name because residents felt that too many places in the area had names that finished with 'up'. But the authorities disagreed and the name stayed.

Goat Island (NSW)   Goat paradise

The Aboriginal name for this island is 'Melmel' meaning 'the eye'. It was first called Cockatoo Island, but later changed, because in the early years of the colony it was used for the purpose of grazing goats.

Goat Island (SA)   Goats for lunch

This island, which is part of Nuyts Archipelago, was named because of the practice of leaving goats on the various islands to supply fresh meat to boat crews.

Goodnight (QLD)   Night whispers

Apparently the captain of a river steamer on the Murray River heard a voice calling 'Goodnight' from the riverbank. Henceforth, that particular spot was called 'Goodnight'.

Goonellabah (NSW)   Local coral

Goonellabah is derived from an Aboriginal word for the native coral tree. The place has had some nicknames, such as Wilsons Ridge and Lovers Retreat.

Gore Hill (NSW)

Named after William Gore who was Provost Marshall to Governor William Bligh. (See Dignitaries, p. 60.)

Gowlland Bombora (NSW)   A wet surveyor

This bombora in Sydney Harbour was named after Commander John Gowlland, who drowned nearby in 1874 while surveying Middle Harbour.

Gowrie (NSW) Scottish hawk?

A locality situated 1.6 kilometres west of New England Highway, about 29 kilometres south of Tamworth, Gowrie is a name of Scottish origin reported to have been bestowed after a place in Northern Ireland; although, another view claims it may be derived from an Aboriginal word, 'gauri', meaning 'down of the eagle-hawk'.

Grabowsky Range (WA) Climbing Poles

A mountain range in northern central Western Australia, named after Ian Herman Grabowsky, a Scottish immigrant of Polish origin, who arrived in Australia in 1919 and became a pioneer of Australian air transport. (See Polish Names, p. 168.)

Gracetown (WA) Young, graceful and brave

Named in commemoration of 16-year-old Grace Bussell for her bravery in saving approximately fifty passengers from the wrecked steamship, the *Georgette*, by riding her horse into the surf. (See Horses, p. 95.)

Grampians (VIC) Back to Tacitus

The word 'Grampian' was given to a mountain range by the explorer Major Thomas Mitchell after the Grampians in his homeland of Scotland. But the word 'Grampian' is itself a misspelling of 'Mons Graupius', which is the name of a battle in the area given by the first-century historian Tacitus. It was transcribed as 'Mons Grampius' by a sixteenth-century historian and from there became the Scottish and then the Australian 'Grampians'. (See Mistakes and Apocrypha, p. 139.)

Graveyard Hollow (NSW) Unmarked grave

A short and unremarkable watercourse runs through this area, the name of which dates back to the 1880s. The name is locally used, and legend has it that the descendants of a pioneering family are buried here.

Green Cape Lighthouse (NSW) More white than green
This lighthouse on Green Cape, from which it takes its name, was the first cast concrete lighthouse tower constructed in Australia.

Green Toad Tea Garden (NSW) Multifunctional
This small reserve in suburban Sydney is the original site of a house known as 'Ellerslie', and later as 'The Green Toad Tea Gardens'. The owners erected ten rustic teahouse shelters in 1933 and during the war years it was hired by the army as a convalescent hospital.

Greenway Reserve (NSW) Lowly beginnings
This small reserve commemorates Francis Greenway, an architect who was transported to Sydney in 1814 for forging a document. In 1816, he was appointed civil architect and assistant engineer, subsequently designing many government buildings that came to be considered gems of early Australian colonial architecture.

Gregory National Park (NT) Scratches in the bark
This park in the Victoria River area is named after the explorer, Augustus Gregory. In 1855, with six companions, he undertook a yearlong expedition in this area. A tree on the boundary of the national park bears his original inscription.

Grey Mountain (TAS) No loss of pigment
This mountain was named after the British prime minister of the same name, not from its colour, as is often assumed. (See Mistakes and Apocrypha, p. 139.)

Gruszka Lake (WA) Polish mappers
Named after the soldier, George Gruszka, who discovered the lake in 1961 while on a mapping mission. (See Polish Names, p. 168.)

Gudarra (WA) Started as a sore foot
Gold was discovered here in 1892 and the place was known

as Sore Foot Rush, a reference to the tired limping diggers who first arrived. Then for unknown reasons, it changed to Paddington, and subsequently to Gudarra, of unknown meaning and source. (See Changed Names, p. 30.)

Guilderton (WA)   Golden wreck
Named after the Dutch ship *Gilt Dragon*, which was wrecked nearby in 1656 with a loss of thousands of guilders from Holland. (See Ship Names, p. 183.)

Gulgong (NSW)   Picture of money
Known affectionately during the 1960s and 1970s as the town on the $10 note, the name Gulgong is thought to have been taken from the Wiradjuri people's word for 'deep waterhole'.

Gumley Gumley (NSW)
A suburb of Wagga Wagga. (See Double Names, p. 101.)

Gunbower (VIC)
From an Aboriginal word 'gambowra', thought to mean 'twisting'. (See Aboriginal Names, p. 11.)

Gundagai (NSW)   Flash Jack
Originating from the name of a station owned by Ben Warby in 1826 and thought to be derived from an Aboriginal word variously said to mean 'going up stream' and 'sinews', this town was immortalised in Banjo Paterson's poem 'Flash Jack from Gundagai'. (See Literary Names, p. 123.)

Gunn (NT)   Territorian experience
A suburb of Palmerston named after Jeannie Gunn who wrote *We of the Never Never*, about her experience of the Northern Territory. (See Literary Names, p. 123.)

Gwalia (WA)   Welsh town lives again
Discovered in 1896 and backed by Welsh finance, this goldfields town is best known for its 'Sons of Gwalia' mine. Gwalia is Welsh for Wales. It later turned into a ghost town

until new mining technology reopened it with modern open-cut workings.

Gympie (QLD)   Tent city and the promise of gold

Gympie is situated on the Mary River in south-eastern Queensland in a thriving farming area. The town's history dates back to the mid 1800s when it was a goldmining town. Gold was discovered there in 1867 by James Nash, and within a few weeks thousands of hopeful prospectors flocked to the district, followed by those who were keen to set up commercial endeavours around the goldfields. Tents sprang up everywhere. At first the area was called 'Nashville', after John Nash, but the name was soon changed to 'Gympie', after a local species of stinging tree, called 'Gimpi-Gimpi' by the local Aborigines. The tents soon gave way to buildings, roads were built and Gympie found its place on the map.

GERMAN NAMES

There are scores of places around Australia whose names indicate a German heritage. Most of these are found in South Australia, where the population included a greater number of people of German descent than any other state.

When World War I broke out, governments were concerned that so many places and landscape features had names with a link to the then national enemy. In 1916, South Australia moved to remedy this. A report of the state's Nomenclature Committee stated, 'The time has now arrived when the names of all towns and districts in South Australia which indicate a foreign enemy origin should be altered, and that such places should be designated by names either of British origin or South Australian native origin.' In all, sixty-nine name changes were effected, many of the new names being borrowed from Aboriginal languages. As if to make an extra point, some of the new names were inspired by the war itself — especially battles, such as Verdun, the Somme, the Marne, and generals, such as Haig and Allenby. Some were overlooked, the most notable being the state capital, Adelaide.

The following table lists South Australian locations whose German names were changed during World War I. Some of the original names (in italics) were later restored.

Original German name	New name
Bartsch's Creek	Yedlakoo Creek
Basedow, Hundred of	Hundred of French
Berlin Rock	Panpandie Rock
Bethanien	Bethany
Bismarck	Weeroopa
Blumberg	Birdwood
Blumenthal	Lakkari
Buchfelde	Loos

German Names

Original German name	New name
Cape Bauer	Cape Wondoma
Carlsruhe	Kunden
Ehrenbreitstein	Mount Yerila
Ferdinand Creek	Ernabella Creek
Friedrichstadt	Tangari
Friedrichswalde	Tarnma
Gebhardt's Hill	Polygon Ridge
German Creek	Benare Creek
German Pass	Tappa Pass
Germantown Hill	Vimy Ridge
Gottlieb's Well	Parnggi Well
Grunberg	Karalta
Grunthal	Verdun
Hahndorf	Ambleside
Heidelberg	Kobandilla
Herrgott Springs	Marree
Hildesheim	Punthari
Hoffnungsthal	Karawirira
Homburg, Hundred of	Hundred of Haig
Jaenschtown	Kerkanya
Kaiserstuhl	Mount Kitchener
Klaebes	Kilto
Klemzig	Gaza
Krawe Rock	Marti Rock
Krichauff	Beatty
Kronsdorf	Kabminye
Langdorf	Kaldukee
Langmeil	Bilyara

Original German name	New name
Lobethal	Tweedvale
Mount Ferdinand	Mount Warrabillinna
Mount Meyer	Mount Kauto
Muller's Hill	Yandina Hill
Neudorf	Mamburdi
Neukirch	Dimchurch
New Hamburg	Willyaroo
New Mecklenburg	Gomersal
Oliventhal	Olivedale
Paech, Hundred of	Hundred of Canna Wigra
Petersburg	Peterborough
Pflaum, Hundred of	Hundred of Geegeela
Rhine (north), Hundred of	Hundred of Jellicoe
Rhine (south), Hundred of	Hundred of Jutland
Rhine Hill	Mons
Rhine River North	The Somme
Rhine River South	The Marne
Rhine Villa	Cambrai
Rosenthal	Rosedale
Schomburgk, Hundred of	Hundred of Maude
Seppelts	Dorrien
Schreiberhau	Warre
Siegersdorf	Bultawilta
Steinfeld	Stonefield
Summerfeldt	Summerfield
Vogelsang's Corner	Teerkoore
Von Doussa, Hundred of	Hundred of Allenby
Wusser's Nob	Karun Nob

H

Hahndorf (SA)   Remembering the captain

A quiet agricultural town that has kept its distinctive European character, established by its early German settlement, Hahndorf was first settled by fifty-two German families who arrived in 1839. The settlers wanted to remember the captain of the Danish ship *Zebra*, which brought them from their homeland. They called it 'Hahndorf' after Captain Dirk Hahn. During World War I, because of anti-German feeling, the name was changed to 'Ambleside', but the original name was restored in 1936. (See Changed Names, p. 30, German Names, p. 83.)

Halloran (NSW)   Carving up the land

Located on the Central Coast of NSW, this area was named in memory of Henry Halloran, a surveyor and town planner who owned large parcels of land in NSW. He was one of the first land developers in the state.

Halls Gap (VIC)   Curiosity led to a wild romantic glen

The area known as Halls Gap is a mountain range first discovered by Europeans in 1836. The highest mountain of the range was named 'Mount William', after the British monarch of the time,

King William IV. Having done his duty for the British crown, Major Thomas Mitchell then named the whole range 'The Grampians' after the Grampians of his homeland, Scotland. A few years later the pastoralist Charles Browning Hall drove a large herd of cattle to Port Phillip Bay in Victoria. He was disappointed to arrive and find the market already overstocked. Hall decided to follow Major Mitchell's route to find a suitable run, with ample feed and water and no squatters on it. When he found the area around the place that later took his name, he was struck by its untouched beauty. He seems to have established friendly relations with the local indigenous people. One day his curiosity led him to follow some native tracks leading in towards the ranges and this is how he happened to discover a 'wild romantic glen'. It was this gap in the range that was soon after to be known as 'Halls Gap'.

Hamelin Pool (WA)

Named after explorer Nicolas Baudin's second-in-command, Emmanuel Hamelin. (See French Names, p. 73.)

Hanging Mountain (NSW)   Steeper than steep

This mountain traces its name back to the stock route to the Bendethera goldfield that passed over it. The steep, almost overhanging, north-eastern slopes have white ash trees growing at almost 90 degrees to the face of the mountain, giving the appearance that they are hanging.

Hanging Rock (VIC)   Not a good place for a picnic

An area made famous by Joan Lindsay's book *Picnic at Hanging Rock*, which was made into a film of the same name by Peter Weir in 1975. (See Literary Names, p. 123.)

Harbord (NSW)   Seaside honour

This seaside suburb in Sydney, allegedly honours the maiden name of Lady Carrington, the wife of Lord Carrington, Governor of NSW from 1885 to 1890. In recent years there have been moves afoot to change the suburb's name to Freshwater.

Harness Cask (NSW)   Parcel pick-up

This oddly named locality in the northern coastal region of Bellingen is said to be derived from the fact that the harness of a dead bullock was put into an empty cask here to be picked up at a later date.

Harry McCormick Arboretum (NSW)   Greenie

This pleasant roadside rest area within Mathoura State Forest is named after Henry David (Harry) McCormick (1914–89). McCormick was the Mathoura Sub-District Forester from 1946 to 1979 and one of the longest serving foresters at Mathoura. He was ahead of his time in encouraging tree plantings and in testing new tree species. He planted the trees in this area in 1978. The arboretum is situated on the western side of the Cobb Highway, about 100 metres south of the intersection with Morris Street, Mathoura. There are about thirty species of trees suited for dry climates planted in the arboretum.

Harveys Return (SA)   Lazarus

This treacherous cove on Kangaroo Island was favoured by a group of sealers led by Joseph Murrell. They were a group of tough characters, known as 'sea rats', who lived here before the first official landing thirty years later in 1836. The name comes from one of the sealers, called Harvey, who made it to shore after his mates had given him up for dead.

Hassans Walls (NSW)   Hideout

It has been said that when the road to Lithgow was being built by convict labour, an Egyptian named Hassan escaped and hid under the walls. An escarpment and Lithgow suburb are named in his memory in this locality, near a series of sandstone hills and escarpments south of Lithgow overlooking the valley of Coxs River. Some good lookouts are established on it.

Hattons Bluff (NSW)   Burn and bluff

This mountain was named after Bill Hatton who, according to local legend, used to stay there when he visited from Sydney.

The legend says the local Aboriginal people would burn his hut down while he was away and he bluffed that he would build a concrete and stone place.

Hawks Nest (NSW)   Navigation aid
This town, on the northern shores of Port Stephens, takes its name from a large hawk's nest on the bank of the Myall River, which was used as a navigation aid.

Headley Tarn (NSW)   Gained an 'a' and a lake
This lake was named by Reverend J Milne Curran after Charles Hedley, who accompanied Milne Curran on an 1896 expedition to study glaciers in the area.

Hell Hole (NSW)   Unexplained extremism
The intriguing name has never been fully explained. One story tells of a tractor accident that killed the driver, but this not does seem, of itself, to warrant the extreme name.

Herods Gate (TAS)   Unholy role
This is the name of a pass. Herod's Gate is a north-facing gate in the old city of Jerusalem, so named because it led to the place where King Herod's palace used to be. Herod was a ruler of ancient Galilee and is best known for his role in the crucifixion of Jesus. (See Tasmanian Names, p. 199.)

Hexham (NSW)
Named after a place in England. (See Nostalgia, p. 151.)

Hill Sixty (NSW)
This hill near Inverell is named after a Gallipoli battle scene in 1915. (See War Names, p. 218.)

Hobart (TAS)   Keeping the French out
The town that became the capital of Tasmania was named after Robert Hobart, Secretary of State for War and the Colonies at the time of its settlement. Its beginnings were far from auspicious: it was settled for the sole purpose of preventing the French

from doing the same. A party of forty-nine, including thirty-five convicts, was sent, under the leadership of Lieutenant John Bowen, to establish a settlement on the Derwent River. By the third decade of the nineteenth century Hobart was a thriving port, serving Tasmania and Bass Strait, as well as sealers and whalers who sailed the southern oceans. It has never completely lost its reputation for a certain unruly frontier spirit. One unnamed historian is cited as having written of its early population: 'Such a hard and inhospitable place inevitably attracted a certain kind of person. By the 1820s the flotsam and jetsam of the world, men seeking refuge from the law or seeking isolation from other human beings, has been drawn to the shores of the island.' (http://walkabout.com.au) (See Dignitaries, p. 60.)

Holbrook (NSW)   Nostalgic bread

This town near Albury has been known by a number of names since the 1820s. In 1824 the explorers Hume and Hovell named it Friday Mount and Camden Forest. In 1836, it was known as Therry's Billabong after the Reverend John Therry. By 1838, it was using the name Ten Mile Creek. In 1858, it took the name Germanton because of the high number of German immigrants who had settled there; and this was officially gazetted in 1876. There are still some excellent bakeries in Holbrook, apparently a legacy of the German past. At the start of World War I, because of anti-German feeling, the name was changed to Holbrook, after a famous submarine captain, Lieutenant Norman Holbrook. (See Changed Names, p. 30, War Names, p. 218.)

Holdsworth (NSW)   And then there were five

An avenue in Muswellbrook named after a local family who sent seven sons to World War II, two of whom died. (See War Names, p. 218.)

Home Rule (NSW)   A reminder

A village north of Mudgee, named by Irish miners to remind

themselves as well as others of their demands for Home Rule for Ireland. The village features as the O'Connell Town in *The Miner's Right* by Rolf Boldrewood. (See Literary Names, p. 123.)

Honeymoon Gap (NT)   From temple to honeymoon
Honeymoon Gap was the second name of the area first called 'Temple Bar Gap', in 1871. In 1942 a newly married young couple planned to spend their honeymoon at the Gap. The army gave Bob, the husband, a week's leave and rations (mostly tinned goods) and the couple borrowed a car and a tent. But the car didn't get them far. It had a flat battery, so the bridal couple got a push start and managed to make it over the 17 kilometres of rough road to the Gap. It rained most of the week. Some of their friends went out to visit the honeymooners. It was at that time that the area was renamed 'Honeymoon Gap'.

Hong Kong (SA)   A Chinese connection
This place on Eyre Peninsula marks the locality where a Chinese shepherd lived and worked, but whether the name honours him or his homeland is not clear.

Hope Islands (QLD)   Hope springs eternal
Apparently, Cook's *Endeavour* had struck a reef and was taking in water but managed to reach some small islands. They were so named because of the hope that inspired the crew to arrive safely.

Hope Valley (SA)   Eternal optimist
This valley was named by one William Holden whose house there burnt down in 1851. His intention was to indicate that he had not lost hope in the future.

Horseshoe (WA)   Lucky
Originally this gold mining area was known as 'Horseshoe Bend' because the first leases filled the spine of a horseshoe-shaped ridge there. It later became 'Horseshoe'. (See Horses, p. 95.)

Horsham (VIC)   Visitor comments

In 1895 Mark Twain, visiting American novelist wrote, 'Horsham sits in a plain which is as level as a floor . . . grey, bare, sombre, melancholy, baked, cracked, in the tedious long droughts, but a horizonless ocean of vivid green grass the day after a rain' (*Readers Digest Illustrated Guide to Australian Places*, 2003). (See Literary Names, p. 123.)

Houtmans Abrolhos Islands (WA)   Eyes wide shut

Abrolhos is derived from the Portuguese 'Abre olhos', meaning 'Look out!' Frederick de Houtman, sailing from Holland to the Spice Islands in 1619, sailed his ship among the reefs and islands off the west coast of 'New Holland' and gave them this name after the similarly named rocks off the coast of Brazil. The warning, however, did not work, as two ships were subsequently wrecked there.

Howlong (NSW)

Named after a two-horse race that went for 160 kilometres, in 1876. (See Horses, p. 95.)

Hue Hue (NSW)

A road crossing at Morrisset. (See Double Names, p. 101.)

Hughenden (QLD)   Greener pastures

Following Burke and Wills' ill-fated expedition from Melbourne to the Gulf of Carpentaria in 1861, William Landsborough checked the area out and praised the grass-covered plains of the Hughenden area. Four cattlemen subsequently raced to secure pastures. The first to drive his herd into the Jardine Valley was Ernest Henry who called his station Hughenden Manor after the home of his English maternal grandfather. The town then took this name.

Humbug Scrub Wildlife Sanctuary (SA)   Unpopular

In the mid 1840s an area of wild country was settled by a couple of squatters called Paddy and Mary Gavan. Mary would occasionally come to town for supplies and was forever asked 'how she liked living in that desolate place'. Mary Gavan always replied, 'I call it a humbug.' From this discontented source was coined a name that has endured to today.

Humpty Doo (NT)   Humpty who?

The locality of Humpty Doo is named after the homestead originally called 'Umpity Doo' and changed to 'Humpty Doo' in the postwar years. Three versions of the origin of the name have been recorded. One is from the word 'umpty', an army slang term used in 1917 to refer to the dash when reading morse code. A second comes from W Hatfield's *I Find Australia* (1943), which refers to 'Humpty Doo Station' and mentions that the name is derived from the colloquialism 'everything done wrong or upside down'. The third is from Elsie Masson's book *Untamed Territory* (1914) in which reference is made to the picturesque 'Umdidu', transcribed by a journalist in 1953 into 'Umdudu'. This was understood to be an English-language rendition of an Aboriginal word for 'a popular resting place'.

Hundred of Milne (NT)   A taste of feudal

The area of land called the 'Hundred of Milne' lies south of Darwin. It was named in 1871 along with a dozen or so other 'Hundreds', a concept that originates from the English local government feudal approach to the subdivision of land between the village and the shire. In Australia, it was mostly a feature of the division of land in South Australia and the Top End of the Northern Territory. The name 'Hundred' itself dates back to William the Conqueror and Edward I. It is believed that a 'Hundred' was the land occupied by a group of people who provided one hundred warriors for the national army. Under Edward I, they were deemed to consist of 'a hundred hides of land'. The hide was believed to be an area of about 30 acres, measured by means of a leather thong and probably the forerunner to the surveyor's chain. Ten families of freemen made a 'Tithing' and ten tithings made a 'Hundred'. In the parts of Australia where this system was adopted, 'Hundred' meant an area of approximately 100 square miles (62 square kilometres).

Huon River (TAS)   Not pine

Named in 1792 by French explorer Bruni D'Entrecasteaux after his captain, Huon de Kermadec. (See French Names, p. 73.)

Hyden (WA)   Getting smaller

A small wheat belt town that lies 336 kilometres south-east of Perth, famous for the nearby Wave Rock. The town's name is a funny corruption of Hydes Rock, which was named after a local sandalwood cutter. When the Lands Department printed it out, the name became Hyden Rock, and since has become known as Hyden.

HORSES

Horses played a crucial role in the early settlement of Australia. No doubt because of the settlers' dependence on and fondness for their horses, many place names memorialised these valued creatures. The following places are named, or believed to have been named, after horses, or at the very least, have some horsy connection. Certainly, being an explorer's horse was a risky business so a little immortality was no doubt well deserved.

In the days before motor vehicles, explorers and pioneers rode on horseback or walked. Many places were named after friends and politicians, the travellers obviously having an eye to the benefits that this would provide on returning to civilisation. But some also took the opportunity to name places after their trusty steeds. This recognised the important role that horses played in making these trips possible. When Burke and Wills were struggling through to the Gulf of Carpentaria, they made the effort to name Billy's Creek after Burke's favourite horse Billy. Like Burke and Wills, Billy perished in the outback. When Angus McMillan explored the Gippsland Lakes region early in 1840, he came upon a large swamp. In a letter written in 1853, McMillan recorded that on 18 January 1840, 'we followed this river [Mitchell River] up until we came to a large morass, to which I gave the name of Clifton's Morass, from the circumstances of my having nearly lost in it, from its boggy nature, my favourite horse Clifton.' It was hazardous being an explorer's horse, but at least a few gained a little recognition.

Place name	State/territory	Story
Badger Creek	VIC	Named after a settler's horse that got bogged in the creek.
Belli Park	QLD	Named by a surveyor after his favourite horse.
Bennett Springs	SA	Named by explorer J McDouall Stuart in 1861 after the death of one of his horses.

Horses

Place name	State/territory	Story
Billys Creek	NT	Named after explorer Burke's favourite horse.
Bottle and Glass	QLD	One theory is that the names were those of two horses that were used by Cobb and Co.
Briseis Mine	TAS	Named after the 1876 Melbourne Cup winner.
Cliftons Morass	VIC	Named by Angus McMillan after his favourite horse.
Dayboro	QLD	Previously called Terror's Creek, allegedly after a prized Arab stallion whose name was actually 'Terah'.
Doctors Creek	QLD	Named after a horse purchased from a horse doctor.
Gracetown	WA	Named in commemoration of 16-year-old Grace Bussell for her bravery.
Horseshoe	WA	Originally known as 'Horseshoe Bend' because of the horseshoe-shaped ridge there.
Howlong	NSW	Named after a two-horse race.
Jardell Island	NSW	Named after a mare that had trained at a local racecourse.
Marvel Loch	WA	Named after the horse that won the 1905 Caulfield Cup.
Maryborough	QLD	Named after Mary, the wife of the Governor of NSW, when the horses drawing her carriage bolted and caused a collision in which she died.
Mount Ainslie	NSW	Named after a British army officer of this name who fell from his horse and broke his neck at this site.
Mount Destruction	WA	Named by Ernest Giles in 1873 because it was here that all his horses died.

Place name	State/ territory	Story
Norseman	WA	Named by the gold discoverer, Lawrence Sinclair, after his horse.
Tarcoola	SA	Named after the winner of the 1893 Melbourne Cup.
Tumble Down Dick	NSW	This name is said to commemorate a blind horse that fell down a hillside to its death.
Williamstown	SA	This area was traded to a Scot for a mob of horses and named after the owner's eldest son.

I

Illawarra (NSW)   Five islands

This was the Aboriginal name for the area that early explorers and settlers referred to as the 'five islands district'. (See Aboriginal Names, p. 11.)

Illawong Bay (NSW)   Water views

This bay in Sydney's Warringah Shire is appropriately named, as 'Illawong' is a local Aboriginal word said to mean 'view of the water'.

Ima Ima (WA)

A pool west of the Tanami Desert. (See Double Names, p. 101.)

Impeesa Reserve (NSW)   Wide awake

This reserve goes by the Zulu name for Baden Powell, the founder of the scout movement. 'Impeesa' means 'wolf that never sleeps'. The scouts have a large training area on land adjoining the reserve.

Inglewood (VIC)   Reminder of home

Located 45 kilometres north-west of Bendigo, Inglewood's reputation is largely historical, dating back to the gold rush days of the 1850s and 1860s. The area of Glenalbyn was owned by the Reverend William Hall, who was born near Inglewood Forest in England. Because the area reminded him of his birthplace, he renamed it 'Inglewood'. Apart from the gold rushes, the area is famous for the 1862 fire that destroyed half the town including ten pubs, in 30 minutes.

Inman Valley (SA)   From the river to the valley

The river from which this valley takes its name was first sighted in 1837. It was named after South Australia's first Inspector of Police, Henry Inman. The area boasts the first recorded discovery of glaciation in Australia.

Innisfail (QLD)   Irish romance

A town some 80 kilometres south of Cairns, named after the 'romantic name for Ireland'. In 1879, an enterprising Irishman, Thomas Henry Fitzgerald, named his property 'Innisfail'. The name became the official name of the town in 1910. Given the significant role of the Irish in the history of the area, the name was considered very appropriate. In fact, one of the town's earliest major landholders was James Quinn, the Bishop of Queensland, who used the names of twelve nuns when purchasing large tracts of land in the area.

Inverell (NSW)   Romantic swans

This name is said to be of Gaelic origin, meaning 'meeting place of swans'. It was first called 'Byron', after the Romantic poet, whose works were popular at the time. The local indigenous name of the area is said to be 'Gree Gree'.

Iron Baron (SA)   A right royal mineral

This is a modern iron ore mining town on the Eyre Peninsula. It is one of a complex of iron ore mining operations including Iron Knob, Iron Monarch, Iron Princess, Iron Prince, Iron Queen, Iron Chieftain, Iron Knight and Iron Duchess. With each discovery of the region's iron deposits, a regal title has been given, Iron Baron being one of the series. (See Royalty, p. 175.)

Ironpot Creek (NSW)   A rocky shape

This watercourse is apparently named after a rock formation that it flows past, which has the shape of an iron pot.

Irrawang (NSW)   The wine starts here

This locality near Gloucester took the same name as that of the homestead of James King, who arrived from Scotland in 1827. He is said to be the first producer of wine in Australia.

Irvington (NSW)   Well-known local

A locality situated east of the town of Casino, named after Clark Irving, a prominent settler in the area.

Isisford (QLD)

Named after the Isis River, the name of the River Thames as it runs through the town of Oxford, England. (See Nostalgia, p. 151.)

Isle of Condemned (TAS)   End of the road

The convicts who were deemed the worst in the penal colony were sent to this island and gave it its name. (See Pessimistic Names, p. 165.)

Isobel Bowden Ridge (NSW)   A ridge in recognition

This ridge in the Blue Mountains is named after Isobel Bowden, who died in 1986. She was a schoolteacher, conservationist, local historian, writer and botanical illustrator who lived in the area.

Ithaca (QLD)

Named by Governor Bowen after the Greek Island where his wife was born. (See Antiquity, p. 6.)

Ivanhoe (NSW)

Named after the novel of the same name by Sir Walter Scott. (See Literary Names, p. 123.)

DOUBLE NAMES

Many place names across Australia, except for Tasmania, are formed as doubles and often draw notice for this curious fact. Indeed, the made-up name for any hypothetical or mythical locality way out west is 'Woop Woop'. Some of the double names are well known, for example, Curl Curl, a suburb on Sydney's northern beaches, Bungle Bungle, a mountain range in Western Australia, Mooney Mooney, a creek and bridge near Gosford, NSW, Wagga Wagga, a city in south-western NSW. What is not so well known is that there are in fact over three hundred such double names. Nearly all are Aboriginal in origin; they name anything from a mountain range to an abandoned waterhole, and interestingly, there is none beginning with the letters A, F, Q or S.

A selection appears below.

Name	State/ territory	Geographical feature
Balla Balla	WA	A river near Port Hedland.
Bli Bli	QLD	A town near Maroochydore.
Boono Boono	QLD	A national park near Tenterfield.
Calle Calle	NSW	A bay near Eden.
Cubba Cubba	NSW	A creek at Taree.
Derry Derry	QLD	A creek south of Mount Isa.
Elong Elong	NSW	A rail siding east of Dubbo.
Gang Gang	NSW	A mountain 20 kilometres south-east of Kiandra.
Gida Gida	NT	A hill north-west of Alice Springs.
Gumley Gumley	NSW	A suburb of Wagga Wagga.
Hue Hue	NSW	A road crossing at Morrisset.
Ima Ima	WA	A pool to the west of the Tanami Desert.
Jinghi Jinghi	QLD	A creek east of Chinchilla.

Double Names

Name	State/territory	Geographical feature
Kara Kara	VIC	A state forest south of St Arnaud.
Kulla Kulla	WA	A hill north of Geraldton.
Merri Merri	NSW	A creek near Walgett.
Millaa Millaa	QLD	A waterfall near Innisfail.
Mugga Mugga	ACT	A locality in Canberra.
Murta Murta	SA	A waterhole in the Flinders Ranges.
Nuga Nuga	QLD	A national park near Rolleston.
Nulla Nulla	QLD	A locality north of Hughenden.
Obi Obi	QLD	A creek near Gympie.
Roo Roo	NSW	A homestead south of Menindee.
Tilla Tilla	SA	A waterhole east of Lake Eyre.
Tucki Tucki	NSW	A state forest south of Lismore.
Walla Walla	VIC	A creek near Warragul.
Wongle Wongle	QLD	A creek north-west of Goondiwindi.
Woy Woy	NSW	A town on the Central Coast.
Yaven Yaven	NSW	A creek near Wagga Wagga.

J

Jabuk (SA)   Afghan connection

Formerly 'Marmon Jabuk', this name is thought to be derived from Pushtu words of the Afghan language ('Mermon' meaning 'Mrs' or 'Lady'; 'Cabuk' meaning 'quick' or 'fast') and named after a favourite camel used by an Afghan driver of a survey team.

Jack Jewry Reserve (NSW)   Far from home

This public reserve in St Marys is named after Jack Jewry, a local boy who was one of the first conscripts to die at the battle of Long Tan in Vietnam. (See War Names, p. 218.)

Jacksons Waterhole (NSW)   Whose water is it?

This locality dates back to the mid-nineteenth century when the waterhole was the centre of court cases about watering rights.

Jacobs Well (QLD)   One well, many Jacobs

By 1872, Jacobs Well was the common name used for a welcome waterhole near the end of a track from nearby Beenleigh, in south-eastern Queensland. There are different theories as to the origin of the name. One is that the area was named after the

Jacob's Well in the Bible, which honoured Jacob, son of Isaac (*Book of Genesis:* Chapter 29: Verses 1, 2 and 10).

Another theory claims it was named after the eldest son of Johann Gottlieb Gross, a pioneer and early settler who it is said found a well while hunting and fishing with friends. Another theory says that Jacob was an engineer on a steamer working between Brisbane and Southport when they ran out of water for the boilers. Jacob went ashore, dug in the sand and found good water. The well was then cased with timber and used by various boating people.

Yet another story is that, in the early 1800s, a group of settlers was attacked by Aborigines and while they were struggling home with one of their number badly wounded, they noticed a wet patch on the sand which, on digging, revealed good, clear water. As the discovery was regarded as an act of God's grace, the well was given its biblical name. (See Antiquity, p. 6.)

Jaffa Vale (TAS)   Not the chocolate kind

This valley was named after Jaffa, a coastal town that was the historic port to ancient Israel. (See Tasmanian Names, p. 199.)

Jamisontown (NSW)   Like father, like son

This neighbourhood was named after Thomas Jamison who was granted 1000 acres in 1805 by Governor Philip Gidley King. He'd arrived with Governor Arthur Phillip as Surgeon's Mate on the First Fleet ship *Sirius*, in 1788, progressing to Surgeon-General of NSW in 1803. Thomas Jamison returned to England, where he died in 1811. His son, the surgeon Sir John Jamison, took up his father's grant in 1814, his property eventually covering 6.4 square miles (4 square kilometres) of the area to the south of Penrith.

Jannali (NSW)   Good-looking moon

An Aboriginal name for 'place of beautiful moon-rises'.

Jardell Island (NSW)   Equine touch

An island in the waters of the reservoir impounded by Chaffey

Dam near Tamworth, it is named after a mare that had trained at a local racecourse and won $70 000 in prize money. (See Horses, p. 95.)

Jenolan Caves (NSW)   A private hideaway
The name of these spectacular limestone caves is believed to be an Aboriginal word for 'high mountain'. The caves are around 450 million years old and were first discovered by Europeans when, around 1840, a local escaped convict and bushranger became the first white man known to have entered the caves, using them as a hideaway.

Jeparit (VIC)   Small but famous
A tiny wheat belt service town in an area given over to the production of wheat, wool, barley and oats. The first European in the immediate vicinity was explorer Edward Eyre who camped at nearby Lake Hindmarsh in 1838 while searching for an overland route from Melbourne to Adelaide. Jeparit was gazetted in 1889 from an Aboriginal word said to mean 'home of small birds'. The area is noted for its early settlement by German Lutherans who came across from South Australia in the 1880s. It is also known for bushranger Dan Morgan, and the rabbit plague that struck the area in the late 1870s. Another local curiosity was the discovery, in 1916, of a subterranean chamber with a hidden entrance. Inside were German newspapers dating back to 1914. It was assumed to be the refuge of escapees from the POW camp at Langwarrin. More recently it was famous as the home of Sir Robert Menzies, Australia's longest serving prime minister. Jeparit also received some notoriety when it was used as the setting for Peter Carey's 1985 novel *Illywhacker*. (See Literary Names, p. 123.)

Jericho (QLD)   All that's needed now is Joshua
A tiny rural settlement more than 1000 kilometres west of Brisbane, Jericho was first surveyed by explorer Major Thomas Mitchell in 1846. One of the early settlers in the area was a man

named Harry Jordon, after whom the nearby Jordon River was named. A local person jokingly suggested that as the township was on the Jordan River, it should be named Jericho. (See Antiquity, p. 6.)

Jerilderie (NSW)   Terms of endearment?
The name of this town is claimed to be from the Wiradjuri word, 'djirriildhuray', for 'reedy place', though legend has it that the wife of an early settler whose name was Gerald called him 'Gerald dearie'. The town gained notoriety when the Kelly gang held it for two days in 1879, capturing the police station, cutting the telegraph wires and robbing the bank. (See Aboriginal Names, p. 11.)

Jiggi (NSW)   Local myth
This village near Lismore is a mythological site, its name reputedly coming from the Wiyabal word 'jigay', meaning 'cat bird'.

Jimmy Bancks Creek (NSW)   Ginger Meggs at home
Named after Jimmy Bancks, the cartoonist who created Ginger Meggs. As a child he lived in Hornsby at the top of the catchment and followed the creek when raiding a local orchard or swimming. Through the series *Ginger Meggs*, Bancks described settings, characters and adventures of his own childhood (Ollif, *There Must Be a River*, 1975). (See Literary Names, p. 123.)

Jinghi Jinghi (QLD)
A creek east of Chinchilla. (See Double Names, p. 101.)

Joe Hyam Reserve (NSW)   Fighting fire
Located near Nowra and named in memory of a much respected fireman honoured for his community service.

Jordan River (QLD)   Crossing the Jordan
This small river is located near the town of Jericho and is named after the biblical Jordan River that runs through Syria, Lebanon, Israel and Jordan. (See Antiquity, p. 6.)

Judgement Rock (TAS)   Seated on high
Named by Matthew Flinders because of its resemblance to an
elevated seat. (See Topograhy, p. 196.)

Julian Rocks (NSW)   In the family
These prominent rocky islands near Cape Byron, consisting
of 'Juan', 'Julia' and 'Baby Rock', have attracted many myths
and legends. One tells that Nguthungulli, the all-seeing creator,
placed the rocks where they are now.

Junee (NSW)   Talking frogs
This town some distance from Cootamundra is apparently
named after an Aboriginal word that means 'speak to me' or
'green frog', but which one and why this name in this area has
never been made clear.

DUAL NAMES

Dual naming enables and encourages traditional Aboriginal
names to co-exist with European names. In recent years, as a
result of the concerted efforts of the NSW Aboriginal Languages
Research and Resource Centre and the Geographical Names
Board of NSW, a policy of dual naming has been implemented.
Its purpose is to ensure that Aboriginal place names are
preserved and to promote awareness of Aboriginal heritage
and custodianship. The project is the outcome of extensive
community collaboration and consultation. The selection
below relates to places around Sydney Harbour, with more dual
naming planned for regional areas of the country (*Placenames
Australia*, 2005).

Non-aboriginal name	Aboriginal name
Bennelong Point	Dubbagullee
Blues Point	Warungareeyuh
Bradleys Head	Boorghee

Dual Names

Non-aboriginal name	Aboriginal name
Campbells Cove	Meeliyahwool
Careening Cove	Weeyuh Weeyuh
Chowder Bay	Gooree
Chowder Head	Gooragal
Darling Harbour	Tumbalong
Dawes Point	Tar-ra
Elizabeth Bay	Gurrajin
Elizabeth Point	Jerrowan
Farm Cove	Wahganmuggalee
Fort Denison	Muddawahnyuh
Lavender Bay	Gooweebahree
Macleay Point	Yurrandubbee
Middle Head	Gubbuh Gubbuh
Mosman Bay	Goram Bullagong
Mrs Macquaries Point	Yurong
Potts Point	Derrawunn
Shark Island	Boowambillee
Sydney Cove	Warrane

K

Kabbibada Gully (NSW) Stony gully
Located in the country town of Wellington, the gully formed by this small waterway is named after the local Wiradjuri word 'kabbibada', meaning 'limestone'.

Kakadu (NT) Preserving for the future
Listed as a World Heritage site both for its natural and cultural heritage, the name 'Kakadu' is said to come from the Aboriginal Gagudju language. No meaning has been ascribed to it.

Kalamata Grove Walkway (NSW) Pass the olives
This small park near Blacktown owes its name to the district in Greece that is internationally famous for its picturesque olive groves and superb quality olives.

Kalgoorlie (WA) Gold!
Australia's last gold rush town was discovered in 1893 by Thomas Flanagan, Dan Shea and 'Paddy' Hannan when they camped by Mount Charlotte. The town's name comes from one of two local Aboriginal names: 'koolgooluh', meaning 'edible silky pear' and 'kalgurli', meaning 'a twining vine-like plant'.

Kara Kara (VIC)
This is a state forest south of St Arnaud. (See Double Names, p. 101.)

Kareela (NSW)   Kite weather
A suburb on the southern shores of Oyster Bay in Port Hacking, the name 'Kareela' comes from the Aboriginal word 'kari-kari', meaning 'fast'. The reference may be to the strong southerly wind in the region.

Karrawarra Reserve (NSW)   Green it is
In 1894 James Miller inherited land from his father and subsequently, in 1912, changed the farm's name from 'Willow Farm' to 'Karrawarra'. When the land was subdivided, a reserve was created. According to the family's oral history, the word comes from the Wonarua language and means 'green'.

Kata Tjuta (NT)   Many queens in one place
The phrase means 'many heads' in an indigenous language. It refers to a group of more than thirty rounded red conglomerate masses of rock rising out of the desert plain, about 500 kilometres south-west of Alice Springs. Some of the rocks are bunched closely together with only narrow precipitous crevices between, while others have been rounded and polished by the wind and are more spaced apart. The collection of rocks was formerly known as 'The Olgas', named in 1872 by the explorer Ernest Giles after Queen Olga. She was known for supporting scientific expeditions in the latter part of the nineteenth century. Her husband, King Karl of Württemberg, Germany, had honoured Giles's sponsor, Baron Ferdinand von Mueller, by making him a hereditary baron. Like nearby Uluru, Kata Tjuta has great spiritual significance for local indigenous people.

Katamatite (VIC)
Named from an Aboriginal word 'catamateet', meaning 'of local creek'. (See Aboriginal Names, p. 11.)

Katoomba (NSW)   Cascades
Said to be derived from an Aboriginal name variously spelt 'kedumba', 'kedoombar' and 'godoomba' and meaning 'falling waters'.

Keepit Dam (NSW)   You can keep it!
A major dam on the Namoi River, the name of which is thought to mean 'keep it', a derogatory remark about the apparent worthlessness of the adjacent pastoral run.

Keerrong (NSW)   A fox is a fox in any language
This small village near Lismore was known as 'Fox Ground' by early settlers but in 1897 the named was changed to 'Keerrong', said to mean 'flying fox'.

Keith (SA)   Starting out as monstrous
Formerly known as Mount Monster after a nearby large granite outcrop, the town was officially proclaimed in 1889. At the time, Lord Kintore was the Governor of South Australia. Kintore's Scottish home was called 'Keith Hall' and he was also known as Lord Keith. Another explanation is that the name comes from the eldest son of a local grazier named Sir Lancelot Stirling but there is not strong evidence to support such a claim. The Lord Kintore explanation is backed by both his presence in South Australia at the time and the tendency to honour governors by naming towns after them.

Kermandie River (TAS)
A tributary of the Huon River, named after Huon de Kermadec. (See French Names, p. 73.)

Kiandra (NSW)   Golden skis
The site of one of Australia's most hectic gold rush towns as well as its first ski club, Kiandra was originally called 'Giandara' or 'Giandarra Plain', a term reputed to mean 'sharp stone' in the language of the local Aborigines.

Kilkivan (QLD)   Rise and shine and change your name
The Kilkivan area was settled in the 1840s and takes its name from a property that was established around that time. The earlier name was 'Rise and Shine', named after a gold reef was discovered at nearby Mount Neurum in 1868.

Killara (NSW)
Named from a local Aboriginal word meaning 'permanent, always there'. (See Aboriginal Names, p. 11.)

Killarney (QLD)
Named after the Irish town of the same name. (See Nostalgia, p. 151.)

Killcare (NSW)   Leave your worries behind
The 'Killcare Estate' was the name given to a 1916 subdivision. The name was chosen to promote the area as a place to forget your worries.

Kilroo (SA)   Keeping it short
Sometimes a name is what it appears to be. This one is an abbreviation of the words 'killing kangaroos'.

Kimba (SA)   Burning bush
The belief is that 'kimba' is a local Aboriginal word for 'bushfire', a notion embraced by the local council in the area, which has chosen a burning bush to be the area's emblem.

King Davids Peak (TAS)   Once a king
This is a bluestone mountain. David ruled for forty years as king of ancient Israel. (See Tasmanian Names, p. 199.)

King George Sound (WA)   The sound of George
A large inlet on the south-western coast of Western Australia named after King George III in 1791. (See Royalty, p. 175.)

King Sound (WA)   Not royalty
Named after the explorer Captain Phillip Parker King. (See Exploration Names, p. 66.)

Kingscote (SA)   Make up your mind

This was the first settlement in South Australia. It was first named Angas after George Fife Angas, one of the colony's founders, but after a dispute, it was renamed after Henry Kingscote, another of the founders. (See Changed Names, p. 30.)

Kissing Point (NSW)   A kiss is just a kiss

Various interpretations exist for this place name. One is rather poetic: the boats 'kissed' the rocks as they came ashore. Another is that the place was a popular picnic spot, where the men would receive kisses after carrying ladies ashore. A third was that the men of a picnic party fell asleep in the hot sun and were only roused by the kisses of the ladies of the party.

Kitchener (NSW)   Your country needs you

This town near Cessnock was named after Earl Kitchener, British Secretary of State for War during World War I. (See War Names, p. 218.)

Klemzig (SA)   A different hemisphere

A suburb of Adelaide, named in 1838 after the German name of a village in Poland. (See German Names, p. 83, Polish Names, p. 168.)

Kuranda (QLD)   Natural home

Situated in the hinterland behind Cairns in Far North Queensland, the name comes from a local Aboriginal word thought to mean 'village in a rainforest'.

Kuring-gai National Park (NSW)

Named after the land situated to the north of Sydney, this Park first opened in 1894. The name is said to come from the local Aboriginal people, the Gurrangai, for whom it held great cultural and spiritual significance.

Kurri Kurri (NSW)

There's agreement that this name is Aboriginal in origin, perhaps meaning 'the first' or 'the beginning' but beyond this, the name is a mystery.

Kwinana (WA)   A wreck comes to life again

Located south of Fremantle, this industrial town takes its name from the local Aboriginal word for 'young woman' or 'pretty maiden'. The name was borrowed from a freighter, *SS Kwinana*, which was wrecked on Cockburn Sound in 1922. During a storm, she was blown ashore to the place where she rests today. The area soon became known as 'Kwinana', and was formally named in 1937. (See Ship Names, p. 183.)

L

La Perouse (NSW) Man vanishes, suburb remains
A suburb of Sydney named after the Count of La Perouse,
a famous navigator who eventually disappeared following a
shipwreck. (See French Names, p. 73.)

Laanecoorie (VIC)
Named from two Aboriginal words — 'languy' meaning 'resting
place' and 'coorie' meaning 'kangaroo'. (See Aboriginal Names,
p. 11.)

Lake Caddiwarrabirracanna (SA) Size is everything
On the Oodnadatta Trail, this small place has the distinction of
having one of the longest place names in Australia — and is
not surprisingly referred to familiarly as 'Lake Caddi'. For other
very long place names, see Mamungkukumpurangkuntjunya
Hill (SA), p. 128 and Warrawarrapiralilullamalulacoupalynya
(NT), p. 212.

Lake Galilee (QLD) Promises, promises
One of two lakes in the Lake Galilee wetlands, this lake was
named after the Sea of Galilee in Israel. (See Antiquity, p. 6.)

Lake Leg of Mutton (SA)   Pass the gravy

This lake at Mount Gambier was so named because it was thought to resemble a leg of mutton. (See Topography, p. 196.)

Lake Ophion (TAS)   Snakes alive

This lake was named after a huge serpent in Greek mythology. (See Tasmanian Names, p. 199.)

Lake Petrarch (TAS)   Unrequited love

This lake was named after the Italian Renaissance poet. (See Tasmanian Names, p. 199.)

Lake Salome (TAS)   Head on a platter

This lake was named after Salome, who was the mother of Jesus' apostles, James and John. (See Tasmanian Names, p. 199.)

Lake Sidon (TAS)   Ancient pleasures

This lake was named after Sidon, an important city in ancient Phoenicia criticised in the Old Testament as being a place of idolatry and materialism. (See Tasmanian Names, p. 199.)

Lake Thor (TAS)   Sore all over

This lake was named after the god of war in Norse mythology. (See Tasmanian Names, p. 199.)

Lake Wendouree (VIC)   Go away!

An unconfirmed story says this lake was originally called 'Yuille's Swamp' after a squatter by the name of William Yuille. He named it 'Wendouree', believing that this was the name by which it was known locally by the Aborigines of the area. In fact, when they said 'Wendouree', they were telling him to go away.

Lamb Island (QLD)   Not the kind you roast

This island was named after the English poet and essayist, Charles Lamb, a friend of the poet Coleridge. (See Literary Names, p. 123.)

Lancelin (WA)   Man of maps

Derived from the name of the nearby Lancelin Island, named by the French expedition in 1801 honouring P F Lancelin, author of *The World Map of Sciences* and works on the planetary system and analyses of science. (See French Names, p. 73.)

Largs (NSW)   Battles last long in the memory

Named after a locality in Ayrshire, Scotland, famous for the battle of Largs fought in 1620.

Laura (SA)   Poetic inspiration

A small country town established in 1872, and much loved and written about by the poet C J Dennis, who wrote a famous poem 'Laura Days' on the occasion of the town's golden jubilee in 1932. (See Literary Names, p. 123.)

Leda (WA)   Swansong

Leda is named after the brig *Leda*, which brought settlers to the new colony in 1830. Leda means 'swan', an appropriate name for a ship that brought colonists to the settlement on the Swan River. (See Ship Names, p. 183.)

Legges Camp (NSW)   Games and recreation

This area was named after Henry Legge, a game hunter who regularly camped on the eastern shore of Boolambayte Lake, which subsequently became a popular recreation area.

Leichhardt (NSW)   Mysterious German

This suburb of Sydney was named after Ludwig Leichhardt, a German explorer, scientist and geologist who came to Australia in 1842. He went on many explorations, especially in Queensland and the Northern Territory, and eventually disappeared, giving rise to many stories and legends — from mutiny to murder to floods — about what happened to him. But his fate remains a mystery. Leichhardts's expedition from Sydney to Darwin and his subsequent mysterious disappearance inspired Patrick White, arguably Australia's greatest novelist, to base his great novel *Voss* on the explorer. (See Exploration Names, p. 66, Literary Names, p. 123.)

Lemnos (NSW)   Cutting up the cook

Lemnos Parade is a street in the suburb of Cooks Hill, which was subdivided in 1915 after the Dardanelles campaign. (See War Names, p. 218.)

Lenswood (SA)   Echoes of war

This town in the Adelaide Hills was named in 1917, during World War I after the French town Lens had been devastated in the war. The name symbolised the slaughter and remembered many of the local men who were serving or had been killed there. (See War Names, p. 218.)

Leonora (WA)   The trinity

There is agreement that the explorer John Forrest was responsible for the name 'Leonora' in the late 1860s, during his search for the Leichhardt expedition. The question is — which Leonora? One report says she was Forrest's niece. Another suggests she was his 'lady friend'. A third says the Leonora in question was the wife of the WA governor of the time. It is not impossible, though not very likely, that she was all three.

Level Post Bay (SA)   Water level

This bay, located at Lake Eyre, was named by C W Bonython, who erected a water level gauge post in the bed of the lake.

Linger and Die (NSW)   Way to go — not!

Linger and Die was once a part of the booming goldfields near Avoca, in Victoria, at the foot of the Pyrenees Ranges.

Little Oaky Creek (NSW)   Strong as oak

A creek named after one or both of the casuarina trees that grow in the area, either the Belah (*Casuarina cristata*) or the Bull Oak (*Casuarina luchmannii*), as each is known as an 'oak'.

Liverpool (NSW)   Oldest of the Macquarie towns

A city on Georges River, the oldest of the 'Macquarie Towns', Governor Lachlan Macquarie named it in 1810, after Robert

Banks Jenkinson, second Lord of Liverpool, later Prime Minister of Great Britain.

Llandilo (NSW)   A saintly past

A village in Penrith, named after the Welsh town of Llandilo Faw. The origin of the name was credited to Saint Teilo, who lived in the sixth century. Until 1895 the district had been known as 'Terry Brook', after Samuel Terry, who was granted 950 acres in the area in 1818. When the land was divided up in 1895, the present name was introduced. 'Llan' means 'a church or enclosure'.

Lobethal (SA)   Enemy perils

In 1842, a community of eighteen German families arrived at the Onkaparinga River, in the Mount Lofty Ranges, where they established the settlement of Lobethal. Led by their pastor, they held an open-air service of thanksgiving, where he read out a passage from the Bible: 'And on the fourth day they assembled themselves in Lobethal; for there they blessed the Lord.' Drawing on their Bible, they named the place Lobethal.

The name endured until 1918, when the political events of World War I got in the way. At that time, South Australia had sixty-seven so-called 'enemy place names', mostly German, reflecting the early settlement demographic of the state. Lobethal was deemed 'German', one might infer in this case because of the origins of the settlers, rather than the actual name. A report was commissioned by the government of the day to advise on the change of names from enemy countries to names mostly derived from Aboriginal languages. The report (Parliamentary Report No 66, 7 November 1916) was called 'Nomenclature Committee's Report on Enemy Place Names' and was passed by Parliament on 10 January 1918. At that time, Lobethal officially became known as 'Tweedvale'. Seventeen years later, with improved German relations with the Commonwealth, the government of the day reversed the names of three places to their original names. One of these was Tweedvale, which returned to its original 'Lobethal'. (See German Names, p. 83)

Lochinvar (NSW) — Scottish touch
Named after Sir Walter Scott's poem. (See Literary Names, p. 123.)

Lock (SA) — Sent to war
A small country community that was deprived of its young men during World War I. The town was named after Corporal Albert Lock, a local citizen who was killed in action in Belgium in 1917. (See War Names, p. 218.)

Lockhart (NSW) — Green grog
A town near Wagga, originally known as 'Greens Gunyah' and later renamed 'Lockhart' in 1897. 'Greens Gunyah' was so named because a Mr Green, the earliest settler, had a grog shop there, on the Urana to Wagga Wagga stagecoach route.

Log of Knowledge Park (NSW) — Miners meeting
This park in Kurri Kurri has an interesting history. It is believed that the name comes from the early mining years of the district when miners held gatherings at the 'Log of Knowledge', a place where discussions took place about mining issues.

Londonderry (NSW) — Home away from home
When Thomas Kendall was granted 30 acres of land in 1831, he called the property Londonderry, presumably after his home.

Lonesome Section (QLD) — Roo paradise
This is an isolated area of Expedition National Park. Difficult to reach, it is a sanctuary for many species of kangaroo and wallaby. (See Topography, p. 196.)

Long Island (NSW) — Long and bespectacled
This island in the Hawkesbury River is named for its shape. It is also called 'Spectacle Island' by some locals, apparently because it looks like a pair of glasses.

Long Mountain (NSW)   Long but not long enough
This mountain is so called because it is long for a mountain of its height, but too isolated and not long enough to be called a 'range'.

Long Sleep Plains (NSW)   Sweet dreams mate
These plains between Port Augusta and Whyalla allegedly derived their name from a local story about a wagon driver who fell asleep on a journey between those two places.

Longreach (QLD)   Long arm of the law
Featured in Rolfe Boldrewood's novel, *Robbery Under Arms*, the town is said to have taken its name from the 'long reach' of the nearby Thomson River. (See Literary Names, p. 123.)

Longueville (NSW)   A noble duke
A neighbourhood near Hunters Hill and Lane Cove in Sydney, said to have been named after a French nobleman, the Duc de Longueville.

Longworth Park (NSW)   Community-minded
Named after William Longworth, who came to Australia with his father, an engineer with the Australia Agricultural Company. He settled on the Karuah River and made generous contributions to the local community.

Look At Me Now Headland (NSW)   All dressed up
This headland north of Coffs Harbour has an interesting story behind it. Allegedly, one overdressed immigrant, who was trying to impress some local girls with his fine clothes, was bespattered by some galloping horses on the nearby black soil plain. When he returned, his clothes evoked a plaintive, 'Look at me now'. And the name stuck.

Lord Howe Island (NSW)   Soaking up the noble sun
A popular holiday destination, this island lying in the Pacific Ocean north-east of Sydney was named after Admiral Lord Howe.

Lovett Bay (NSW)   Love it or leave it
A bay within Pittwater not far from Scotland Island, named after a local settler, John Lovett, in 1836.

Lucky Bay (WA)   Lady luck
Named by Matthew Flinders in 1802 when his ship the *Investigator* sheltered there during a storm. The ship was steered for the mainland where a sandy beach was sighted and was graced with good fortune, for it entered a sheltered bay and cast anchor.

Lucy Hill (NSW)   We love Lucy
This hill near Weddin was named after Lucy Cobcroft, who was born in 1896, the daughter of the local primary school headmaster, and later became known for her community work, especially during the war.

Luddenham (NSW)
Named after a district in Kent. (See Nostalgia, p. 151.)

Lugarno (NSW)   A little bit of Europe
A Sydney suburb reputedly named after a lake on the borders of Italy and Switzerland, although why such a name was chosen is not clear.

Lunatic Hill (NSW)   You'd have to be crazy
An area of Lightning Ridge, the famous opal-mining area, so named, local legend has it, because the ground is so hard you'd have to be crazy to dig there.

LITERARY NAMES

All the names in the following selection have a literary connection.

Place name	State/territory	Literary connection
Alpha	QLD	A small township where many of its streets honour English poets.
Ardath	WA	A townsite possibly named after the novel *Ardath, the Story of a Dead Past* by Marie Corelli.
Artarmon	NSW	Possibly a corruption of the Greek name Artemon. There were five Greeks with the name Artemon, all of whom had some literary connection. This allusion may well be apocryphal as evidence exists to confirm that Artarmon was named by William Gore after his home in Ireland.
Ashbourne	SA	Named after the village where Thomas Moore wrote the poem 'Lalla Rookh'.
Auburn	SA	The birthplace of the poet C J Dennis, author of *The Songs of a Sentimental Bloke*.
Avoca River	VIC	Named after the poem 'Sweet Vale of Avoca' by Thomas Moore.
Bagdad	TAS	From *The Arabian Nights*.
Boolaroo	NSW	This town was depicted as 'Boomaroo' in novels by Paul Radley.
Boomerang Park	NSW	Named after the author John Houlding who wrote under the name of 'Old Boomerang'.
Byron Bay	NSW	Conventionally thought to be named after the famous romantic poet Lord Byron; however, it was named before his time.
Cape Rose	WA	Named after Rose de Freycinet, who published a journal known in English as *A Woman of Courage*.
Cervantes	WA	Presumably named after the Spanish writer.

Literary Names

Place name	State/ territory	Literary connection
Chaucer Street	NSW	A street in the Hunter Valley named after the English poet.
Come by Chance	NSW	Banjo Paterson was intrigued by the name.
Dimboola	VIC	Made famous by the play of the same name by Jack Hibberd.
Dog on the Tuckerbox, Gundagai	NSW	Named after the anonymous poem 'Bullocky Bill', later echoed in the poem 'Nine Miles from Gundagai'.
Enngonia	NSW	Associated with a number of bush balladeers including Will Ogilvie and Henry Lawson.
Eurunderee	NSW	Poet Henry Lawson went to school in Eurunderee, which features in his poem 'The Old Bark School'.
Gundagai	NSW	Featured in Banjo Paterson's poem 'Flash Jack from Gundagai'.
Gunn	NT	Named after Jeannie Gunn who wrote *We of the Never Never*.
Hanging Rock	VIC	An area made famous by Joan Lindsay's book *Picnic at Hanging Rock*.
Home Rule	NSW	The village features as the O'Connell Town in *The Miner's Right* by Rolf Boldrewood.
Horsham	VIC	American novelist Mark Twain visited here in 1895.
Ivanhoe	NSW	Named after the novel of the same name by Sir Walter Scott.
Jeparit	VIC	The town was used as the setting for Peter Carey's 1985 novel *Illywhacker*.
Jimmy Bancks Creek	NSW	Named after Jimmy Bancks, the cartoonist who created Ginger Meggs.
Lamb Island	QLD	Named after the English poet and essayist, Charles Lamb.
Laura	SA	A small country town much loved and written about by the poet C J Dennis.

Place name	State/territory	Literary connection
Leichhardt	NSW	Named after the explorer Ludwig Leichhardt, whose disappearance inspired novelist Patrick White in his great novel, *Voss*.
Lochinvar	NSW	Named after Sir Walter Scott's poem.
Longreach	QLD	Featured in Rolf Boldrewood's novel, *Robbery Under Arms*.
Milton	QLD	Named after the seventeenth-century English poet.
Moulamein	NSW	Mentioned in a poem by Banjo Paterson.
Murdoch	WA	Named after Sir Walter Murdoch, a prominent Australian academic and essayist.
Nowhere Else	SA	Inspired well-known writer Dorothy Hewitt to name her play *Nowhere*.
Oberon	NSW	Suggested by a local resident who sought inspiration from the king of the fairies in Shakespeare's *A Midsummer Night's Dream*.
Orpheus Island	QLD	From Greek mythology.
Paroo River	NSW	Featured in a poem by the same name by Henry Lawson.
Pindars Peak	TAS	Named by explorer John Hayes in 1794, after the nom-de-plume of the English poet John Wolcott, who had taken the name from the Greek poet Pindar.
Port Lincoln	SA	The writer Colin Thiele was a schoolteacher in the district and his novel *Blue Fin* is set in the area.
Sarah Island	TAS	Described in Marcus Clarke's novel *For the Term of his Natural Life*.
Sherwood	QLD	Named after Sherwood Forest in the story of *Robin Hood and his Merry Men*.
Sleeping Beauty Mountain Range	TAS	Named after the fairytale of the same name.
Strzelecki Track	SA	Believed to be the inspiration for Captain Starlight in Boldrewood's novel *Robbery Under Arms*.

Literary Names

Place name	State/ territory	Literary connection
Temora	NSW	Named after a poem in *The Poems of Ossian* by James Macpherson.
Tennyson	QLD	Named after the famous poet Lord Tennyson.
Tortilla Flats	NT	Named after the novel by John Steinbeck.
Warwick	QLD	Named after a character in a novel by Lord Lytton, *The Last of the Barons*.
Waverley	VIC	Named after Sir Walter Scott's 'Waverley' novels.
Woodend	VIC	Nearby is the famous Hanging Rock, which featured in the Joan Lindsay novel *Picnic at Hanging Rock*.

M

Macintyre River (NSW)   A matching pair

A perennial stream forming part of the headwaters of the Darling River, it was originally named the Dumaresq River. The current name, as well as that of Macintyre Falls, honours Peter Macintyre who was the overseer at a local property.

Macquarie (NSW)

Named after Lachlan Macquarie, Governor of NSW. (See Dignitaries, p. 60.)

Macquarie Harbour (TAS)   Risky entrance

When James Kelly and four companions sought shelter from a storm in their open whaleboat *Elizabeth*, they dubbed the anchorage 'Macquarie' in honour of the NSW Governor, Lachlan Macquarie. It is now known to be one of the largest natural harbours in the world, its famously risky entrance being appropriately known as 'Hells Gates'.

Madmans Track (WA)   Insane no more

Now a well-formed road in the Pilbara but originally considered a track that only a madman would use — 1500 kilometres of mulga and sandy wasteland. (See Topography, p. 196.)

Magnetic Island (QLD)   Mind your compass

Captain James Cook named the island 'magnetic' apparently having noted that 'the compass did not traverse well when near it'. Since then, no one else has noted this. These days the island is affectionately known as 'Maggie' by many locals. (See Topography, p. 196.)

Maguires Creek (NSW)   Pioneer cedar cutter

This creek is named after a local pioneer, Joseph McGuire (also spelt Maguire), who came to the Richmond River with the first cedar cutters in 1842, and built the first hut at Tintenbar on Emigrant Creek north-west of Ballina.

Maiden Gardens (NSW)   A floral tribute

These gardens in the Sydney suburb of Auburn are named after the Director of the Sydney Botanic Gardens (now the Royal Botanic Gardens) from 1896 to 1924. His views were sought for developing planting styles for the state's public gardens, including the abattoir area that is now part of the Olympic site.

Maisie Talbot Gully (NSW)   The farmer's wife

In 1936 Maisie Talbot, her husband Jack and their son James took up 112 acres at Mount White near Gosford. She led the life of a farmer's wife of that time, which included a lot of hard work such as carrying water from this creek, which rises on the property.

Maitland (NSW)   Good behaviour

This city on the Hunter River near Newcastle was named after the Earl of Lauderdale. The original settlement is said to have been established by 'eleven well-behaved convicts'.

Mamungkukumpurangkuntjunya Hill (SA)

Listed in the *South Australian Gazetteer* as the longest official name in Australia, the name is thought to mean 'where the devil urinates', derived from the local Pitjantjatjara language. For other long place names, see Lake Caddiwarrabirracanna

(SA), p. 115 and Warrawarrapiralilullamalulacoupalynya (NT), p. 212.

Manly (NSW)   Boys own

Situated 4 kilometres north-east of Sydney on the lower northern beaches, Manly was Sydney's first tourist resort. As soon as the colonial settlers arrived in Sydney, Manly was earmarked for a beachside tourist destination and a quarantine station. Manly was named by Captain Arthur Phillip after his encounter with the confident and 'manly' Aboriginal people of the Kay-ye-my clan who lived in the area.

Mannahill (NSW)   Manna of the Gods

Named after the food that was miraculously supplied to the Israelites after their exodus from Egypt. The notion behind the naming was that the area had a good tucker shop. (See Antiquity, p. 6.)

Marble Hill (SA)   Build your bathroom here

An historical town in the Adelaide Hills, it was named after the presence of marble nearby. (See Topography, p. 196.)

Marvel Loch (WA)

A townsite named after the horse that won the 1905 Caulfield Cup. (See Horses, p. 95.)

Maryborough (QLD)   Third-party insurance

Named in 1847 after Mary, the wife of the Governor of NSW, Sir Charles Lennox, when the horses drawing her carriage bolted and caused a collision in which she died. (See Horses, p. 95.)

Mathinna (TAS)   A lost girl

This town was named after a young Aboriginal woman who was found wandering dazed in the bush. She was subsequently cared for by the Tasmanian Governor, Sir John Franklin and his wife Lady Jane Franklin.

MEASURED NAMES

Before Australia changed its measuring system from imperial to metric in the 1970s, many place names included measurements made in 'miles'. Sometimes the measurement is of the feature itself — such as Eighty Mile Beach in Western Australia — and sometimes it is of the distances that explorers and pioneering settlers travelled from other places before reaching the place that they named. This might have been the distance from 'a settler's hut, another creek or a sly grog shanty' (Richards, personal correspondence, undated). There are also places like Fairmile Cove (NSW) that contain the word 'mile' but not as an overt measurement. In the case of Fairmile Cove, the name honours World War II naval veterans who served on the 'Fairmile' naval ships, most of which were built at neighbouring Green Point naval dockyard.

After the introduction of the metric system, some names bore evidence of the change — the 134 Kilometre Bridge and the 136 Kilometre Bridge, south of Darwin (NT).

Many examples of the old 'mile' names are found in Victoria, such as One Mile Creek, Nine Mile Creek, Fifteen Mile Creek and Thirty Mile Creek. No one, however, has suggested changing the existing 'mile' names to their kilometric equivalent. Somehow, even beyond the matter of custom, one suspects these sound better as miles — compare Five Mile Creek to Eight Point Three Kilometre Creek.

Medina (WA)   Arrived by ship

Medina was named after the vessel *Medina*, which arrived at the Swan River Colony in 1830 with fifty-one passengers. The name is believed to be derived from a river on the Isle of Wight. (See Ship Names, p. 183.)

Melbourne (VIC)   Batman without Robin

Melbourne narrowly escaped being named after the explorer,

John Batman, one of the original graziers who settled there. The area was founded by settlers who came from Van Diemen's Land (later Tasmania) and settled on the land of the Kulin people, the indigenous inhabitants at that time. It was officially named in 1835 after the British Prime Minister of the time, Lord Melbourne, whose home was near the village of Melbourne in Derbyshire. The name 'Melbourne' derives from the Old English for 'mill stream' ('mylla burne'). The city and port of Melbourne took off as important centres as a result of the discovery of gold in Victoria in the mid-nineteenth century. At the time of Federation, in 1901, Melbourne was the national capital, but the seat of government moved to Canberra in 1927. (See Dignitaries, p. 60, Nicknames, p. 146.)

Memory Cove (SA) A dangerous place

A cove near Port Lincoln, named by Matthew Flinders in memory of the tragedy of losing two officers and six men in a boating accident on 21 February 1802.

Merino (VIC) Warm coats

The town of Merino in the Western District is named after the Merino Downs sheep station, established in the area by the pioneering Henty family. (See Sheep Names, p. 180.)

Merri Merri (NSW)

A creek near Walgett. (See Double Names, p. 101.)

Messines (QLD) Two steps forward

A town near Stanthorpe named after an Allied victory in World War I. (See War Names, p. 218.)

Millaa Millaa (QLD)

A waterfall near Innisfail. (See Double Names, p. 101.)

Milton (QLD) Literary pretensions

A suburb of Brisbane, named after the seventeenth-century English poet. (See Literary Names, p. 123.)

Mole Creek (TAS)   Now you see it, now you don't

This farming and forestry village is a popular starting place for excursions to the Great Western Tiers, its name describing the area because streams tend to appear and disappear into the ground.

Molonglo (ACT)   A dam is not a damn

The name of a river that was dammed to form Lake Burley Griffin, the word is thought to be derived from an Aboriginal word meaning 'like the sound of thunder'. (See Aboriginal Names, p. 11.)

Monkey Creek Place (NSW)   Monkeys without tails

Local legend claims this place name came from a group of convicts who, as they were building a road, saw strange creatures (koalas) in the trees and presumed them to be monkeys.

Monkey Gully (VIC)   Monkeying around

There is a story that this place name comes from the idea that an escaped monkey from a travelling circus found refuge in the area. However, as the early settlers called koalas 'bears' or 'monkeys', just as they called wombats 'badgers', it is likely that Monkey Gully is named after its koalas. (See Mistakes and Apocrypha, p. 139.)

Monkey Mia (WA)   Whose monkey?

A town on the coast of Western Australia famous for its dolphins, it has been called Monkey Mia since the end of the nineteenth century. Presumably, the name is made up of an Aboriginal word, 'Mia', and the name of a pearling boat, *Monkey*, which used to moor nearby.

Montacute (SA)   Who's cute?

Situated in the Adelaide Hills, Montacute is named after a little town in Somerset. (See Nostalgia, p. 151.)

Montmorency (VIC)   Back to nature

Named after a farm, the Montmorency Estate, which was itself named after the French town where Jean Jacques Rousseau lived. (See French Names, p. 73.)

Mooloolaba (QLD)   Fishy snakes

Derived either from 'mulu' or 'mullu', an Aboriginal word for 'black snake', meaning 'place of black snakes' ('muluaba'). Alternatively, derived from 'mula', which means 'fishing nets'; hence the belief that it means 'place of the snapper fish'. (See Aboriginal Names, p. 11.)

Moulamein (NSW)

This place is mentioned in a poem by Banjo Paterson. (See Literary Names, p. 123.)

Mount Ainslie (NSW)   Who dares wins — or not

After a British army officer of this name who, while on the summit of the mountain, accepted a bet that he could gallop down the steepest part of it. His horse missed its footing and Ainslie fell and broke his neck. He was buried on the spot where he died. (See Horses, p. 95.)

Mount Alexander (VIC)   A Macedonian down south

Mount Alexander was named by Major Thomas Mitchell after Alexander the Great, the fourth-century Macedonian king.

Mount Ararat (VIC)   Resting place

Named after its biblical namesake by Horatio Spencer Wills, a settler who stopped in the place after a rigorous overland journey. He recorded his thoughts in his diary: 'This is Mount Ararat, for like the Ark, we rested here.' (See Antiquity, p. 6.)

Mount Barney (QLD)   What mountain is that?

Some confusion surrounded the name of this mountain and others in the area. It was first called Mount Lindesay, and was later climbed by Captain Patrick Logan who mistook it for Mount Warning, which had been named by Captain James Cook. When he climbed it, he saw Mount Warning from its slopes and realised his mistake. Names were re-allocated at a later date — Mount Lindesay became Mount Barney, after Lieutenant-Colonel George Barney who came to the colony in 1835 with his wife and three children and served in a number of important government positions. (See Mistakes and Apocrypha, p. 139.)

Mount Beerwah (QLD)   Abandonment
According to local Aboriginal legend, 'Beerwah' was the pregnant mother left by her cowardly son to fend for herself as floodwaters rushed across the coastal plain.

Mount Compass (SA)   Don't climb without one
According to local legend, this name originated when Governor George Gawler lost his compass in the area. Mount Compass is known today for its Compass Cup Cow Race, the only one of its kind in Australia.

Mount Desire (SA)   Where there's a will there's a way
This mountain was named by Samuel Parry in 1859 as a symbol of his desire to return home after more than a year of continuous survey work.

Mount Destruction (WA)   No hope left
A mountain named by Ernest Giles in 1873 because it was here that all his horses died and hence all his hopes for success in his expedition were destroyed. (See Horses, p. 95, Pessimistic Names, p. 165.)

Mount Distance (SA)   Miscalculation
This peak in northern South Australia was named by E J Eyre on 1 September 1840 because it was further away than he thought. (See Pessimistic Names, p. 165.)

Mount Fatigue (VIC)   Hard trip
A peak of 586 metres in south-eastern Victoria, it marks one of the points on Strzelecki's desperate eastward march, named by his friend J Lort Stokes in the 1840s to commemorate his Polish friend. (See Polish Names, p. 168.)

Mount Kokeby (WA)   Slip of the pen
The townsite of Mount Kokeby is located in the great southern
agricultural region and named after nearby Mount Kokeby.
However, the spelling is a mistake. Originally recorded as
Mount Rokeby by the Surveyor-General in 1835, it was
mistakenly recorded as 'Mount Kokeby' when a railway station
was opened in 1889. Half a century later, the name of the
hill was changed to match the station name, a choice of
consistency over historical accuracy. (See Mistakes and
Apocrypha, p. 139.)

Mount Kosciuszko (NSW)   A 150-year wait for a 'z'
Australia's highest mountain (2228 metres) was climbed and
named by Polish-born explorer Paul Edmund de Strzelecki after
the Polish hero Tadeusz Kosciuszko, although there is some
doubt as to whether he really made it to the top. Strzelecki spelt
it correctly initially but somewhere along the way, the 'z' was
lost, being replaced finally after much discussion, some 150
years later. The mountain was always known by its anglicised
pronunciation rather than the Polish original. Kosciuszko
National Park and Kosciuszko Creek are similarly named.
There are also three Kosciuszko streets in Melbourne. (See
Polish Names, p. 168.)

Mount Lofty (SA)   The tallest one
The tallest mountain of the Adelaide Hills Range, its summit
at 727 metres was clear enough above the rest of the ranges
to be picked out and named by Matthew Flinders in 1802.
(See Topography, p. 196.)

Mount Nelson (TAS)   Plaque got it wrong
Named in 1811 by Governor Lachlan Macquarie after the
recently deceased British war hero, Horatio Nelson, though a
plaque on the summit incorrectly asserts that it was named
after the ship *Lady Nelson*. (See Mistakes and Apocrypha,
p. 139.)

Mount Olympus (TAS)   Greek and godly

This mountain was named after the home of the supreme Greek gods. (See Tasmanian Names, p. 199.)

Mount Ossa (TAS)   Pssst!

This mountain was named after Ossa, the goddess of rumour in Greek mythology. There is also a Greek mountain of the same name. (See Tasmanian Names, p. 199.)

Mount Oxley (NSW)

Named after explorer John Oxley by explorer Charles Sturt. (See Exploration Names, p. 66.)

Mount Spion Kopje (VIC)   This time, the Boers

A mountain near Myrtleford named after the site of a bloody battle between the Britons and the Boers on a mountaintop in Natal, South Africa, during the Boer War of 1899–1902. (See War Names, p. 218.)

Mount Strzelecki (NT)   Consonant cluster

A peak of 600 metres about 250 kilometres north of Alice Springs in the Crawford Ranges, named in 1860 by John McDouall Stuart. The name Strzelecki is also found in a national park and mountain peaks in Tasmania; in a town in Gippsland, Victoria, and neighbouring ranges; in a creek in South Australia, discovered and named in 1845 by Charles Sturt who was a friend of the Polish explorer. Another creek by the same name is in Jindabyne, NSW. (See Polish Names, p. 168.)

Mount Warning (NSW)   Thunder and lightning

The name, Mount Warning, was given by Captain James Cook in May 1770 during his trip up the east coast of Australia, presumably because of its formidable profile from sea. Located inland from Tweed Heads in northern NSW, its Aboriginal name is 'Wollumbin', which means 'fighting chief of the mountains'. The belief was that thunder and lightning seen on the mountain were fighting warriors, with the wounds of these fights being represented by the landslides that occurred. The fact that it was once an active volcano might explain the basis of this story.

Mount Watch (SA)   What time is it?
A peak in south-east South Australia, it is so named because Robert Leake of Glencoe lost his watch in the vicinity and never found it.

Mud Springs (QLD)   Mud for sale
Under the surface of the dry land lies the huge body of water called the Great Artesian Basin, releasing near-boiling water from specially sunk bores. (See Topography, p. 196.)

Mugga Mugga (ACT)
A locality in Canberra. (See Double Names, p. 101.)

Murdoch (WA)
This Perth suburb was named after Sir Walter Murdoch, a prominent Australian academic and essayist. (See Literary Names, p. 123.)

Murray River (NSW, SA, VIC)
Named by the explorer Captain Charles Sturt after the English statesman, Sir George Murray. (See Dignitaries, p. 60.)

Murrumbidgee River (NSW)   Big man river
The name of this river in southern NSW derives from the local Aboriginal word for 'big river'.

Murta Murta (SA)
A waterhole in the Flinders Ranges. (See Double Names, p. 101.)

Murwillumbah (NSW)   Scratchy sounds
The name of this town, situated on the Tweed River in northern NSW, is said to have been derived from an Aboriginal word meaning 'home of many possums'.

Muswellbrook (NSW)   One for the road
The origin of the name is unclear – it could be a compound

word formed from 'Mussel' and 'Brook' because of the mussels found in the local creek. Alternatively it could have been named for its resemblance to either Muswell Hill in London or Musselburg near Edinburgh.

Situated in the Hunter Valley Region, Muswellbrook has honoured the local wine industry in the naming of its streets. These include Burgundy Street, Cabernet Street, Chablis Street, Chenis Close, Hermitage Place, Isobella Street, Pinot Street and Riesling Street.

MISTAKES AND APOCRYPHA

Place naming is like any other human endeavour, subject to the slips of ignorance, error and misinformation. It is not uncommon for a place name to be given with good intentions but based on partial or mistaken knowledge. Sometimes, when the mistake is discovered, a change of name is effected. Other times, the name is already well established and whether or not it is based on a mistake or is in some way apocryphal, the name lives on in the community that connects with it. Sometimes, the name is mistakenly attributed by subsequent generations.

Place name	State/ territory	Background
Alligator Rivers	QLD	Mistaken belief that the crocodiles that infested the marshes were alligators.
Badger Head	TAS	Named after wombats, which early settlers called badgers.
Binnaway	NSW	Supposedly named as a result of an incident in which one Aborigine cut off another's ear and threw it away.
Bordertown	SA	A misnomer as it is 19 kilometres west of the actual border.
Carseldine	QLD	Named after a family called Castledine, but misspelt.
Como	NSW	Thought to be named after its namesake in Italy but more likely the naming was driven by marketing considerations.
Dorrigo	NSW	Supposed to have been named after a Spanish general but now considered to be a derivation of an indigenous word for stringy bark.
Grampians	VIC	Named after the Grampians in Scotland, but the word 'Grampian' is a misspelling of 'Mons Graupius'.

Place name	State/ territory	Background
Grey Mountain	TAS	Named after the British prime minister, not from its colour, as is often assumed.
Hyden	WA	A funny corruption of Hydes Rock.
Monkey Gully	VIC	Supposedly named after an escaped circus monkey but more likely to refer to the local koalas.
Mount Barney	QLD	Some confusion surrounded the name of this mountain, which was mistakenly identified by different explorers.
Mount Kokeby	WA	The spelling is a mistake. Originally recorded as Mount Rokeby, it was misspelt when a railway station was opened.
Mount Nelson	TAS	Named after Horatio Nelson, though a plaque on the summit incorrectly asserts that it was named after the ship *Lady Nelson*.
Pennant Hills	NSW	Some controversy surrounds the naming of Pennant Hills. It may come from a signalling post stationed there or it could honour Thomas Pennant, an English naturalist.
Pine River	QLD	On mistakenly being directed to the wrong river, explorer John Oxley called this Deception River, but subsequently it came to be known as Pine River.
Rottnest Island	WA	The present name was from a Dutch maritime clerk who interpreted Willem de Vlamingh's reference to 'wooderats' (quokkas) as meaning rats.
St Marys Peak	SA	One view is that the snow on the peak of the mountain has associations with saintliness; however, others claim that there must be some mistake as snow is a rarity on this mountain.

N

Nambucca (NSW)   Some kind of water

Derived from the word 'ngambugka' in the Gumbaynggir language meaning 'crooked river' or 'entrance to the waters'. It is possible that the phrase 'ngambaa baga-baga' was corrupted by white settlers to 'Nambucca'. (See Aboriginal Names, p. 11.)

Nammoona (NSW)   Aptly named

This area of rich farming land, principally for cattle, near Casino is taken from a Bundjalung word, 'ngama', meaning 'breast' or 'milk'.

Naomi Honey Reserve (NSW)   Early conservationist

This reserve on the eastern side of Shelly Beach Road, Bateau Bay, was named after Naomi Honey, who lived in the area for thirty-five years and was well known for her active involvement in community work, especially in conservation.

Narcissus River (TAS)   Love yourself

This river was named after Narcissus, a beautiful youth who fell in love with his own image, in Greek mythology. (See Tasmanian Names, p. 199.)

Narrikup (WA) — Swampy

Located in what is now rich farming land, this place gets its name from an Aboriginal word that is said to mean 'place of the peat swamps'.

Nash Hill (NSW) — The family hill

This hill located near Parkes is named after the Nash family, who were one of the earliest white families to settle in the area. 'Nash's Hill' was first shown on a map that appears to date from the gold rush days.

Nathalia (VIC) — Mysterious European royals

This rural township in northern Victoria was gazetted in 1880. The origins are reputed to have a royal connection, but the details are vague. One story was that a titled European lady gave birth to a daughter named Nathalia in the district in the mid-1870s. Another version of the story is that the town is named after the Queen of Serbia, formerly Natalya Keshko, who married and had a son in the late 1870s. No illumination is offered as to why a rural township in faraway Australia would adopt the name of a queen of Serbia. (See Royalty, p. 175.)

Nebo (QLD) — Good view

The name comes from the Jordanian mountain from which Moses caught his first glimpse of the Promised Land. (See Antiquity, p. 6.)

Nelson Bay (NSW) — Remember Nelson?

This town in Port Stephens may be named after Horatio Nelson or the ship *Lady Nelson*. (See War Names, p. 218.)

Nepean River (NSW) — Honouring admin

Named by Governor Arthur Phillip in 1789 in honour of Evan Nepean, the Under-Secretary of State for the Home Department at that time. Nepean had had a major hand in organising the First Fleet and the administration system for the new colony of NSW. The Aboriginal name is 'Yandhai'.

Neutral Bay (NSW)   Limbo land
So named because foreign ships were required to anchor in the bay in order to deter convicts from trying to escape.

New Norcia (WA)   Not the liqueur
Named in 1846 by Benedictine monk Dom Rosendo Salvado, named after the Italian birthplace of St Benedict. (See Nostalgia, p. 151.)

Nguiu (NT)   Tiwi heritage
Located on Bathurst Island in the Northern Territory, the area was once known as 'the Bathurst Island Mission'. The town is now known by its indigenous Tiwi language name.

Niagara (WA)   Dry wit
A townsite whose name is derived from a nearby waterfall, Niagara Falls, which was named in jest as it only had a total drop of 3 metres and then only after heavy rain.

Nimbin (NSW)   A wise old man in the rock
Various versions of the origins of the town's name exist. According to some, it's an Aboriginal word for 'big stone' or 'place of many rocks'. A Bundjalung word, 'nyimbuny', has very solemn connotations and means 'wise man', 'little man' or 'hobbit-cum-sage'. According to others, the word denotes 'a place where dwells a bearded man in a mountain'.

Nimmitabel (NSW)   Two languages, one town
This name has accrued two equally credible stories. In one, the name is said to be a contraction of the English word 'inimitable'. In the other, the Aboriginal meaning 'the place where many waters start' is given.

No Mistake (NSW)   Positive attitude
So named because there was once a person named McGregor who said, 'There's gold there, no mistake'.

Noltenius Billabong (NT)   Billabong burial

This billabong near Tipperary was named after Johannes Lebrecht Noltenius, an early pioneer. Noltenius was second in charge of the first Northern Territory Gold Expedition of 1872. At the time of his death, he was a member of a mining party, which operated the Daly River Copper Mine, the first commercial copper mining enterprise in the Northern Territory. In 1884 the mine was attacked and all members of the party were killed except for Noltenius, who was wounded, and a companion, who had to leave him to raise the alarm. Noltenius was found a few days later and buried near where he had died, adjacent to the billabong that was named in his honour.

Noonamah (NT)   An all-round good place

In 1941 the army ascribed a series of new names to the new military depots and camps in the Northern Territory. One of these was Noonamah, which was borrowed from the language of the Wagaman Aboriginal people and means 'plenty of tucker and good things'.

Norlane (VIC)   Local honours

Norlane is a residential suburb near Geelong, named in 1947 after Norman Lane, a local serviceman who had been cap-tured at Singapore and died working on the Burma–Thailand Railway in 1943.

Norman Brown Park (NSW)   A spot of Eureka

A reserve on the eastern corner of Water Street and the New England Highway at Greta, this small park commemorates a worker uprising of miners against mine authorities. Norman Brown was the miner killed during the riot at North Rothbury Mine in 1929.

Norseman (WA)   Nordic spirit

A West Australian town named by the gold discoverer, Lawrence Sinclair, after his horse of the same name. Coincidentally, Sinclair was of Nordic descent. (See Horses, p. 95.)

North Rocks (NSW)   Rocks in the north

The name of this Sydney suburb dates back to about 1789 and originates in a massive sandstone outcrop to the north of Parramatta.

Nowhere Else (SA)   Somewhere after all

Located 37 kilometres west of Tooligi on the Eyre Peninsula, it was supposedly named by a party surveying the district who had made their camp here and on returning from a trip had been unable to find the camp. Someone remarked, 'If it's not over the next hill it is nowhere else.' The camp was found and the name preserved. This name inspired well-known writer Dorothy Hewitt to name her play *Nowhere*. (See Literary Names, p. 123.)

Nuga Nuga (QLD)

A national park near Rolleston. (See Double Names, p. 101.)

Nulla Nulla (QLD)

A locality north of Hughenden. (See Double Names, p. 101.)

Nullarbor Plain (SA)   Treeless

Although this barren place enjoys a rich tradition of storytelling for the local Aboriginal people, its name is derived from Latin. 'Nulla arbor' means 'no tree'.

NICKNAMES

It has often been noted that Australians have a tendency to nickname their towns and cities. This is something locals do and then others often adopt the nickname as a point of reference. The nickname is mostly affectionate and is used to show your familiarity with the place or your solidarity with locals or others who are familiar with the place. It occurs mostly in spoken language or informal contexts, with the formal name reserved for official and record-keeping functions.

There are some patterns in the nicknaming process.

Shortening the name and preceding it with 'the'.	The Gong (Wollongong, NSW), the Knob (Yorkeys Knob, QLD), the Loo (Woolloomooloo, NSW), the Roy (Collaroy, NSW).
Reducing two-word place names to one, and preceding it with 'the'.	The Isa (Mount Isa, QLD), the Alice (Alice Springs, NT).
Shortening the name and ending it in 's'.	Adders (Adelaide, SA), Scarbs (Scarborough, WA), Snives (St Ives, NSW).
Adding an 'ie' sound to the first syllable.	Austy (Austinmer, NSW), Bally (Balgowlah, NSW), Birchie (Birchgrove, NSW), Brissie (Brisbane, QLD), Broady (Broadmeadows, VIC), Crowie (Crows Nest, NSW), Erko (Erskinville, NSW), Gippy Highway (Gippsland Highway, VIC), Lonnie (Launceston, TAS), Tassie (Tasmania).
Shortening the name and adding 'o' to the end.	Baulko (Baulkham Hills, NSW), Chippo (Chippendale, NSW), Darlo (Darlinghurst, NSW), Kenso (Kensington, NSW), Rotto (Rottnest, WA), Sevvo (Seven Hills, NSW), Singo (Singleton, WA).
Shortening the name and adding 'ers' to the end.	Tuggers (Tuggeranong, ACT), Sydders (Sydney, NSW).

Other nicknames use different conventions.

Canberra (ACT) has been called 'the bush capital', a partly ironic reference to the fact that a lot of the bush was cut down to make way for the city.

Babylon (Avalon, NSW) and Charlie's Trowsers (Charters Towers, QLD) operate within the tradition of rhyming slang.

County Coogee (Coogee, NSW) alludes to the large British and Irish population that visits the beachside suburb.

Double Pay (Double Bay, NSW) and Posh Point (Potts Point, NSW) allude to the knowledge that prices are high in these affluent suburbs.

Hollywood (Beverley Hills, NSW) alludes to a well-known American landmark.

King's Annoyed (Kings Cross, NSW) plays on two meanings (intersection and angry) of 'cross'.

Melbourne (VIC) has been called 'the Athens of the South' because of its large Greek population.

Nappy Valley (Happy Valley, QLD) alludes to the area's high birthrate.

Rock-Vegas (Rockhampton, QLD) is an offshoot of the nickname Bris-Vegas for Brisbane (QLD).

The North Island (Australian mainland) is a tongue-in-cheek reference by Tasmanians to the mainland, along the model of New Zealand's North and South Islands.

Oberon (NSW) Midsummer theme

When a town was surveyed in the sparsely settled region of Bullock Flats, a local suggested the name 'Oberon' in tribute to the King of the Fairies in Shakespeare's *A Midsummer Night's Dream*. He thought such a name might promote luck and happiness. Nearby hamlet Fish Creek followed this theme and renamed itself 'Titania' in honour of Oberon's wife, effecting a connection between the two small towns. (See Literary Names, p. 123.)

Obi Obi (QLD)

A creek near Gympie. (See Double Names, p. 101.)

Odra (QLD)

A street in the town of Gailes, named after the Polish river. (See Polish Names, p. 168.)

Omeo (VIC)

Omeo is an Aboriginal word for 'mountains'. (See Aboriginal Names, p. 11.)

Onkaparinga River (SA) A right mouthful

This river was originally known by the Kaurna name 'Ngangki

parri' before it was changed to 'Field's River'. Not long afterwards, the new Governor-General decreed that original indigenous names were to be used where possible. So 'Field's River' went back to its original Kaurna name, but the initial 'ng' sound, being hard for English speakers to pronounce, meant that it was called 'Onkaparinga River'.

Oodnadatta (SA)   The last laugh

This name is said to be derived from an Aboriginal word meaning 'excreta' or 'smelly water'. There had been an artesian bore west of the town, known for its foul-smelling minerals. The name 'Oodnadatta' may be a variation of the Aboriginal word for 'shit'. An interesting theory is attributed to author Tim Flannery (Whittaker & Willesee 2002, p. 29). He is quoted as having said, 'Almost all the towns around Australia with variations on the word "coon" . . . actually mean shit . . . Across all the Aboriginal languages and dialects, the word for shit is remarkably common. It looks like in a lot of cases when the explorers came through, their guides had a bit of a joke at their expense telling them that this or that place was called shit water or shit mountain or whatever.' (See Aboriginal Names, p. 11.)

Ophthalmia Range (WA)   Through an eye darkly

This mountain range was named by the well-known explorer Ernest Giles, who dreamed of reaching the West Australian coast from central Australia. He made a number of unsuccessful attempts and was finally rewarded by the sight of the Indian Ocean. On the return trip through the desert, he experienced the dreaded 'Ophthalmia', also known as 'sandy blight' or 'trachoma'. He recorded his plight: 'My eyes had been so bad all day, I was in agony . . . At length, I couldn't see at all.' The expedition came upon 'a range of rounded hills'. He wrote, 'I called this . . . Ophthalmia Range, in consequence of my suffering so much . . . I could not take any observations, and I cannot be very certain where this range lies.' (Giles 1889)

Orara River (NSW)   Fishy story
This river in the Clarence Valley is said to draw its name from a local word that means 'where the perch live'. The stream indeed is rich in fish of many kinds, providing for Aborigines and settlers of the time, and continuing to be plentiful to this day.

Orchard Hills (NSW)   Trees replace frogs
A suburb of the city of Penrith, where orchards were an early feature, and still are, making the name very apt. Originally the area was known as 'Frogmore', the name of a grant given to Mary Putland, a daughter of Governor William Bligh. A meeting of residents in 1910 decided on the name change because there was another Frogmore in NSW.

Orelia (WA)
Orelia is named after the ship of the same name that arrived at Fremantle bringing settlers to the new colony in 1829. (See Ship Names, p. 183.)

Orpheus Island (QLD)   Songster
Situated off the coast between Cairns and Townsville, this island was named in 1887 or 1889 after the flagship of the Royal Navy at the time, which was wrecked in New Zealand with the loss of more than 180 men. Presumably, the HMS *Orpheus* was named after Orpheus of Greek mythology, famous for his songs and verse. (See Literary Names, p. 123.)

Otto Losco Reserve (NSW)   Working man tribute
Located near Parramatta, this name commemorates Ottorino Losco (1920–79), who was employed by Parramatta Council in the Parks Division for more than ten years and was killed in an accident while at work in 1979. Fellow staff arranged a petition requesting council to name the park, near which he had lived, in his memory.

Owens Park (NSW)   Four generations
This name stems from the Owen family name, four generations

of whom had lived in the area. Albert Owens was the head-master of Cranebrook Public School in the very early 1900s.

NOSTALGIA

Other than the indigenous peoples, everyone else in Australia is a 'newcomer'. Many came on boats, as has been pointed out to those who denigrate recent arrivals coming here in search of refuge. As Tim Flannery (1994) points out, there is a great irony in naming places like New Guinea, New Zealand and New Caledonia, and other such 'new' places that we now know to be much older than their namesakes.

The early years of hardship and trial must have made many settlers yearn for home. Understandably, they may have felt transplanted onto the other side of the world. For this reason, as well perhaps as to mark their origins, many place names in Australia are named after places back home.

A selection of these follows.

Place name	State/territory	Origin
Antwerp	VIC	The first settler, Horatio Ellerman, named his property 'Antwerp' after the city in Belgium where he was born.
Appin	NSW	Named in 1811 by Governor Lachlan Macquarie after a small coastal village in Argyllshire in Scotland where his wife was born.
Artarmon	NSW	Said to be named by William Gore, who was Provost Marshall to Governor William Bligh, after his home in Ireland.
Ayr	QLD	Named after a place of the same name in Scotland.
Balcolyn	NSW	Amalgam of the Scottish prefix 'Bal' and the name Colyn.

Place name	State/territory	Origin
Charleville	QLD	Named by the Government Surveyor, William Alcock Tully, after his boyhood home in Ireland.
Clare	SA	Named after the home county of Irishman Edward Gleeson, who established a sheep station in the Clare Valley in 1840.
Dandaloo	NSW	Presumed to have been named after a town in France.
Dover	TAS	Named after the English seaport of the same name.
Eidsvold	QLD	Named by a Scottish family, who had moved to Norway and from there to Australia, where they named their run after a Norwegian village.
Fingal	TAS	Named after an Irish town of the same name.
Glendon	NSW	Named by Robert and Helena Scott after their home in Scotland.
Hexham	NSW	Named after a place in England.
Isisford	QLD	Named after the Isis River, the name given to the River Thames as it runs through the town of Oxford, England.
Killarney	QLD	Named after the Irish town of the same name.
Luddenham	NSW	Named after a district in Kent.
Montacute	SA	Named after a little town in Somerset.
New Norcia	WA	Named after the Italian birthplace of St Benedict.
Perth	WA	Named after Perthshire in Scotland in 1829.
Quorn	SA	Named after the English town of Quorndon.
Raworth	NSW	Named after a place in Suffolk.
River Tamar	TAS	Named after a river in south-western England.

Place name	State/territory	Origin
Ross	TAS	Named by Governor Lachlan Macquarie in 1821 after the Scottish home of one of his friends.
Stroud	NSW	Named after Stroud in England.
Subiaco	WA	Named by Benedictine monks after the town in Italy where their order was founded.
Swansea	TAS	Named after Swansea in Wales by pastoralist George Meredith.
Toronto	NSW	Named after the home city of the 1880 world champion in sculling races.
Trundle	NSW	Named after a suburb of outer London.
Tumby Bay	SA	Named by Matthew Flinders after a parish of his native Lincolnshire.
Wakefield	NSW	Named after Wakefield, Yorkshire.
West End	QLD	A Brisbane suburb, named by the English settlers after the famous West End of London.
Windsor	NSW	Named after the royal town of Windsor on the Thames, England.

P

Palm Island (QLD)   Palms of cabbage?

The town of Palm Island is located on Great Palm Island, the largest of the Palm Island Group. The town was named by Captain James Cook in 1770, because of the large number of cabbage trees that grow there.

Palmers Bay (NSW)   Terra firma

Located near Bulahdelah on the Myall Lake, this bay was named after the lone survivor of the 1880 shipwreck of *Fiona*, who settled in the area.

Palmerston (NT)   The three Palmerstons

In the Territory, there have been three townsites called 'Palmerston' over the years. Palmerston was the name given to the townsite established in 1864 by the first Government resident of the Northern Territory of South Australia, Boyle Travers Finniss, at Escape Cliffs, near the mouth of the Adelaide River. Town blocks were surveyed ready for sale to investors in Adelaide and London. This settlement was abandoned in 1865. The second 'Palmerston' was the town surveyed by George Goyder, the Surveyor-General of South Australia at the time, in 1869 at Port Darwin. This town was officially known as 'Palmerston' until March 1911, when the name was changed by proclamation to 'Darwin'. The third and current 'Palmerston' is the surveyed 'Town of Palmerston', a satellite townsite, 21 kilometres east of the city of Darwin, 'constituted and defined as a new town' in May 1981. The name 'Palmerston' was used for the satellite town, as it retained the name first applied to the northern capital by the South Australian Government in commemoration of Lord Palmerston, who became Prime Minister of Britain in 1855. The 3rd Viscount Palmerston's name, Henry John Temple, has been used in the new satellite town with the naming of a main access, 'Temple Terrace'. Development of the current Palmerston commenced in 1984 and following the exceptional growth of the town, in early 2000 the Palmerston Town Council sought and obtained a change in the name of the municipality to 'City of Palmerston'.

Palmyra (WA)   Ancient influence

Palmyra, meaning 'City of Palms', was a famous Syrian city, a centre of commerce on the trading routes of ancient Europe. It was called Palmyra by the Romans who ranked it fourth in the seven wonders of the ancient world. The name 'Palmyra' for this suburb of Perth was chosen from a local competition and, following its win, the street names were chosen for their association with ancient history in the Middle East region, for example, Zenobia, Cleopatra, Solomon, Aurelian and Antony. (See Antiquity, p. 6.)

Parmelia (WA)   Transport for a governor

Parmelia is named after the first ship to bring settlers to the new colony. It arrived in 1829, and among the passengers were the new governor and his wife, James and Ellen Stirling. (See Ship Names, p. 183.)

Paroo River (NSW)   Wet and dusty

An occasional waterway, as often dry as flowing, featured in a poem of the same name by Henry Lawson. (See Literary Names, p. 123.)

Parramatta (NSW)   A place of firsts

On 23 April 1788, Governor Arthur Phillip and a party of explorers discovered an area at the head of a river, about 25 kilometres from Sydney. In November of the same year, Phillip selected the site for a small fort. A town was laid out two years later, becoming the second oldest colonial settlement in Australia. On 4 June 1791, the town received its present name. Phillip called it by what was understood to be the name that Aborigines used, the meaning of which was said to be 'the place where eels lie down'. The area became Australia's first successful farming settlement. John Macarthur, Australia's first 'pastoralist on a grand scale' began in the area with a grant of 40 hectares. Parramatta is a city of 'numerous firsts' — first consecrated church, first ferry service, first road out of Sydney that led to Parramatta, first public fair. Its population quickly outstripped the population of nearby Sydney.

Pelion Gap (TAS)   Half-man, half-horse

This mountain was named after the home of the centaurs in Greek mythology. (See Tasmanian Names, p. 199.)

Pelorus Islands (SA)   Instrumental islands

These three islets south of Kangaroo Island owe their name to a navigation instrument. A pelorus is an instrument attached to a ship's compass to enable the taking of bearings of landmarks, and the name was given to these islets because they aided navigation in the area.

Pemberton (WA)   Honouring the first settler

The town of Pemberton is located 300 kilometres south of Perth within the south-western forest region. The area was first known among settlers there as Big Brook, which was considered not distinctive enough. The name Walcott was suggested but rejected by the post office. Then a farmer in the area suggested calling the town Pemberton after the first settler in the area in 1862. This name was used from 1916 and gazetted in 1925. (See Changed Names, p. 30.)

Pennant Hills (NSW)   Wave the flag

Some controversy surrounds the naming of Pennant Hills. The most popular theory, although lacking any evidence, is that the name came from a signalling post stationed on a hill from where Sydney and Parramatta could be seen. Another theory is that the name honours Thomas Pennant, an English naturalist with friends in high places, such as Sir Joseph Banks. In September 1800, the area was referred to in correspondence as 'Pendant Hills'. This may have been a mistake or it may have been used in the nautical sense, 'pendant' meaning a tapering flag. The general consensus is that the name Pennant Hills originates in the idea of a place of signalling. (See Mistakes and Apocrypha, p. 139.)

Pennefather River (QLD)   River names

It is on this river that Aboriginal people in 1606 probably first sighted Europeans when a Dutch boat, commanded by Willem Janszoon, arrived there from what was then the Dutch East Indies. The historic river has had a succession of recorded names, including traditional Aboriginal names and Dutch and English names. It was named 'Pennefather' in the last decade of the nineteenth century, after the Controller General of Prisons at the time, who explored the river. The Yupungathi people, whose lands lie in the area, still commonly refer to themselves as 'Conn River' people, though this name is itself an adaptation of the Dutch name, 'Coen', used from the time of the early missionary years in the 1890s. The traditional indigenous names apply rather to specific sections of the river, reflecting the local people's detailed knowledge of their landscape and its spiritual associations. The European practice is quite distinct and involves naming a river, or any entire geographical feature, as one.

Peregian (QLD)

Named after an Aboriginal word for 'emu'. (See Aboriginal Names, p. 11.)

Peron (WA)   No relation, Evita

Named after Francois Péron, the French naturalist who had accompanied explorer Nicolas Baudin's earlier expedition in 1802–03. (See French Names, p. 73.)

Perth (WA)   Scottish influence

The first European to sight the Perth area was Dutch sailor Willem de Vlamingh, who sailed along the coast in 1697. He named the Swan River after noting the large flocks of black swans in the area. But de Vlamingh was not enthusiastic about the region, describing it as 'arid, barren and wild'. The area was explored and chartered by the French in 1801 but a subsequent expedition deemed the Swan River unsuitable as a port. In 1827 a British expedition led by Captain James Stirling considered the potential of the river with some enthusiasm and a settlement was planned; as it turned out, it was the first to be developed entirely by free settlers, with convicts being transported from 1850. In 1829, the Secretary for Colonies, Sir George Murray, instructed the Lieutenant Governor-Designate, Captain James Stirling, to name the settlement after his birthplace, Perthshire, in Scotland. Stirling was not displeased with this, being a Scotsman himself. (See Nostalgia, p. 151.)

Piccadilly (SA)   Let's take a walk

The origin of this place name was suggested in a letter in *The Advertiser* in Adelaide in the early 1860s. It referred to a settler in the area who suggested going for a walk. 'Where shall we go?' she was asked, and received the typical Londoner's reply, 'Let's take a walk down Piccadilly'. No doubt this was said in jest given that the area was far removed from its namesake. The ironic naming may have been balm to the homesick settlers of the times. However, another reading of the name has suggested that it may derive from a Kaurna word that sounds very much like 'Piccadilly'.

POSITIVE AND NEGATIVE NAMES

You can choose the names of your children, pet and even house, but the name of the street you live in is mostly the luck of the draw. There are ways of applying to the local council to effect a name change but it is not a fast process. People are usually stuck with what they get or sometimes, conversely, they are happy with the positive connotations their street happens to have. (See Pessimistic Names, p. 165.)

Below are some examples of 'red-faced roads' and 'smile streets' found in NSW (Lacey, 2003).

Red-faced roads	Smile streets
Alcock Avenue, Campsie	Ace Avenue, Fairfield
Barff Road, Camperdown	Action Street, Greenacre
Bogan Place, Wahroonga	Beauty Drive, Whale Beach
Bogie Lane, Hurstville	Casablanca Avenue, Kellyville
Buckleys Road, Winston Hills	Cheers Street, West Ryde
Cockburn Crescent, Fairfield East	Chick Street, Roselands
Dick Street, Balmain	Dream House Lane, Mosman
Dire Straits Way, Berala	Easy Street, Randwick
Fanny Place, Surry Hills	Magic Pudding Place, Faulconbridge
Gay Street, Castle Hill	Nirvana Street, Pendle Hill
Grose Street, Richmond	Paradise Avenue, Avalon
Hymen Street, Peakhurst	Pleasure Point Road, Pleasure Point
Pitt Town Bottoms Road, Pitt Town Bottoms	Santa Place, Bossley Park
Roots Avenue, Luddenham	Welcome Street, Wakeley
Tuga Place, Glenmore Park	Wonderland Avenue, Tamarama

Pichi Richi Pass (SA)   Careful what you drink
A gap in the lower Flinders Rangers, the name of which derives from a plant with leaves said to be intoxicating.

Picton (NSW)   Meeting at Waterloo
A town south of Campbelltown named after General Thomas Picton under whom Governor Thomas Brisbane had served in the Battle of Waterloo. (See War Names, p. 218.)

Pieman River (TAS)   A pie worth remembering?
There is controversy about just which pieman is remembered in this town's name. The most popular version claims it was Alexander Pierce, who is famously remembered as a particularly poor Hobart piemaker. He was jailed for selling pies unfit for human consumption. He later escaped with several fellow inmates and when eventually caught was found to be in the possession of human remains, the apparent leftovers of a spree of cannibalism. The other pieman in question is a pastry cook, who, at a metre and a half tall, somehow managed to escape from Macquarie Harbour, cross Pieman River and reach the north-western coast — the first European to have managed such a dangerous journey.

Pigs Crossing (NSW)   Oink oink!
This is the place on the Bermagui River where pigs were brought from Cobargo and taken across the river to be loaded onto boats and taken to Sydney for slaughter, or once a year, during the Royal Easter Show, for showing with other animals.

Pilny (QLD)   Battling man
This street in the town of Gailes was named after Pilny in Poland, which is also the word for hardworking, diligent or industrious. (See Polish Names, p. 168.)

Pindars Peak (TAS)   Back to the Greeks
A coastal peak in Tasmania, named by explorer John Hayes in 1794, after the nom-de-plume of the English poet and satirist

John Wolcott, who himself had taken his name from the Greek poet Pindar. (See Literary Names, p. 123.)

Pine River (QLD)   Ending up as pine
In 1823, under instructions to look for a suitable site for a convict settlement, John Oxley sailed north from Sydney. Around Moreton Bay he encountered some castaways living with local Aborigines. They told him about a very large river flowing into the bay, but when one of them tried to take Oxley there, he mistakenly directed him up a smaller river to the north of the big one. The mistake prompted Oxley to call it Deception River, and others to refer to it as Blind River, but subsequently it came to be known as Pine River. (See Mistakes and Apocrypha, p. 139.)

Pingaring (WA)
Located in the great southern agricultural region of the state, the name is Aboriginal, derived from the name of a nearby spring. (See Aboriginal Names, p. 11.)

Pinky Flat (SA)   Pass the pinky
This area of land on the River Torrens in Adelaide seems to have two explanations for its name. It was named either after a small animal called a 'pinky' that inhabited the area, or because during the Depression of the 1930s, the area was used as a camping ground by the unemployed and a cheap wine called 'pinky' was consumed there.

Pitt Town (NSW)
Named after the famous English politician, William Pitt. (See Dignitaries, p. 60.)

Plains of Promise (QLD)   Promises, promises
When Captain J Lort Stokes first saw these open downs from the *Beagle*, he prophesised the creation of a peaceful English countryside and wrote about them in *Discoveries in Australia* (Stokes 1846). More than a century later, the area was mined for uranium ore.

Point Lowly (SA) How low can you go?

Matthew Flinders, who named this point, was disappointed to find it, having hoped that the head of Spencer Gulf would end in a major river leading into the interior. Instead he found 'a projection of low sandy land, and beyond it another similar projection', which he called 'Point Lowly'.

Point Perpendicular (NSW) Steep faces

Point Perpendicular was named by Captain James Cook during his famous voyage to Australia in 1770, presumably because of its almost vertical steep rocky faces.

Pokolbin (NSW) Hot as hell

There are several versions of the origins of this place name. One theory is that 'Pokol' means 'purgatory' or 'hell' in Polish. Another is that it comes from Hungarian, meaning 'a very hot place', and with the influx of settlement in the Pokolbin area in the 1860s after the 1848 uprising in Hungary, this does seem probable. A third claims it is a local Aboriginal word for 'a hot place'.

Poles Diggings (QLD) Another Warsaw

An area of land near Ravenswood, north of Townsville, which was named in the latter part of the nineteenth century because it was owned by a Polish digger, Sygurd Wisniowski, who built a gold mine that he called 'New Warsaw'. (See Polish Names, p. 168.)

Polish Corner (TAS) Meet you on the corner

In Hobart, this street corner was officially named in 1982. The corner of New Town and Augusta Roads, it is the site of the Polish–Australian brotherhood-in-arms monument. (See Polish Names, p. 168.)

Polish Hill River (SA) Polish your hill

East of Sevenhill, Polish Hill River was settled by Polish immigrants in the 1850s. (See Polish Names, p. 168.)

Polonia (QLD)

A street in the town of Gailes, the word is Polish for 'Poland'. (See Polish Names, p. 168.)

Pool of Bethesda (TAS)   Go down low

This body of water was named after the Pool of Siloam (meaning 'sent'), which was a huge basin at the lowest point in the city of Jerusalem. (See Tasmanian Names, p. 199.)

Port Arthur (TAS)

The penal settlement was established by and named after Governor George Arthur in 1830. (See Dignitaries, p. 60.)

Port Lincoln (SA)   Tuna fish

The writer Colin Thiele was a schoolteacher in the district and his novel *Blue Fin* is set in the area, describing the loss of a tuna fishing boat in its waters. (See Literary Names, p. 123.)

Prairie (QLD)   Home on the range

While passing through the area in 1862 William Landsborough was reminded of the flat, featureless plains of North America. He named the area 'Prairie' as a result.

Pretty Sally (VIC)   Pretty in name only

This hill was originally called 'Big Hill'. It was changed to 'Pretty Sally Hill', which was then shortened affectionately to 'Pretty Sally'. Sally's full name was Sally Smith and she operated an illegal grog shanty near the summit of the hill in the 1840s. Far from being 'pretty', she was said to be exceedingly ugly, the nickname being ironic in a typically Australian way.

Prevelly (WA)   A Cretan connection

A township near Augusta, it was named after the monastery of Prevelli on the island of Crete as a tribute to the Greek community who helped servicemen after they had escaped from the Germans. (See War Names, p. 218.)

Princess Royal (WA)

A townsite most likely named after Victoria, Adelaide Mary Louisa, the eldest daughter of Queen Victoria. (See Royalty, p. 175.)

Proserpine (QLD)   Fertile

This rich and fertile area famous for sugar and cattle was aptly named by explorer George Dalrymple after the Roman goddess of fertility, Proserpina. (See Antiquity, p. 6.)

Pyrmont (NSW)   Beautiful spa

Pyrmont is named after a German spa town, Bad Pyrmont. The story goes that in 1806 Captain John Macarthur held a picnic on the peninsula for some visiting English guests. One of the women is said to have remarked that it reminded her of the German spa town.

PESSIMISTIC NAMES

It is easy to forget that those who pioneered Australia as explorers and early settlers encountered great challenges, some of which brought dashed hopes, disappointment and despair. Some of the place names collected here serve as reminders of those days.

Anxious Bay (SA)
Avoid Bay (SA)
Battle Camp (QLD)
Blunder Creek (QLD)
Break Me Neck Hill (TAS)
Bungle Bungles (WA)
Cactus Beach (SA)
Cannibal Creek (QLD)
Cape Barren (TAS)
Cape Catastrophe (SA)
Cape Flattery (QLD)
Cape Grim (TAS)
Cape Tribulation (QLD)
Catastrophe Bay (SA)
Coward Springs (SA)
Dangerous Reef (SA)
Dead Man Crossing (QLD)
Dead Man Gully (QLD)
Dead Woman Dreaming (SA)
Deadmans Dugout (SA)
Death Rock (SA)
Deception Bay (QLD)
Denial Bay (SA)
Desperate Bay (WA)
Devils Peak (SA)
Devils Staircase (VIC)
Disappointment Loop (WA)
Disappointment Reach (WA)

Disaster Bay (WA)
Dismal Plains (SA)
Escape Glen (NT)
Escape Point (WA)
Escape River (QLD)
False Bay (NSW)
Fortitude Valley (QLD)
Gunbarrel Highway (WA)
Hangover Bay (WA)
Hazard Bay (QLD)
Hells Gate (QLD)
Hells Gate (TAS)
Hells Window (VIC)
Hopeless Reach (WA)
Isle of Condemned (TAS)
Isle of the Dead (TAS)
Lake Disappointment (WA)
Lake Massacre (SA)
Little Hell (TAS)
Massacre Inlet (QLD)
Misery Bluff (TAS)
Mount Buggery (VIC)
Mount Carnage (WA)
Mount Deception (SA)
Mount Despair (VIC)
Mount Destruction (WA)
Mount Disappointment (NSW)
Mount Distance (SA)

Pessimistic Names

Mount Hopeless (SA)	Skeleton Point (WA)
Mount Misery (WA)	Slaughter Hill (TAS)
Mount Mistake (QLD)	Starvation Lake (SA, NSW)
Mount Regret (NT)	Suiãde Bay (TAS)
Mount Terrible (SA)	Termination Island (WA)
Mount Treachery (NT)	Terrible Hollow (VIC)
Mount Unapproachable (WA)	The Gaol (TAS)
Murdering Gully (QLD)	Thirsty Point (WA)
No No Hole (TAS)	Thorny Passage (SA)
Point Torment (WA)	Torment Point (WA)
Port Misery (SA)	Useless Inlet (WA)
Punchs Terror (TAS)	Useless Loop (WA)
Repentance Creek (NSW)	Weary Bay (QLD)
Repulse Bay (QLD)	Whirlwind Plains (WA)
Repulse River (TAS)	Worlds End (SA)
Savage River (TAS)	

Q

Quambatook (VIC)

Named after an Aboriginal word for 'rat'. (See Aboriginal Names, p. 11.)

Queens Park (WA)

A suburb whose name was changed in 1911 to honour Queen Alexandra, wife of King Edward VII. (See Royalty, p. 175.)

Queenscliff (VIC)

Queenscliff was named in 1853 in honour of Queen Victoria. (See Royalty, p. 175.)

Quilpie (QLD)   Hot opals

Known for its opal mines and piping hot sulphuric bore water, this town's name is an Aboriginal word, thought to mean 'stone curlew'.

Quorn (SA)

Named after the English town of Quorndon. (See Nostalgia, p. 151.)

POLISH NAMES

Polish immigrants have participated in the settlement and development of Australia and their role is documented in the numerous Polish place names around the continent (Kaluski 1983).

Name	State/territory	Feature	Origins
Copernicus	VIC	Street	In Melbourne, two streets are named after the famous Polish astronomer Nicolaus Copernicus.
Cracow	QLD	Town	The town of Cracow was settled in the 1850s and named in honour of the Polish city, which had made a brave stand for independence in 1846.
Curie	VIC	Street	Named after the famous Polish-born scientist Marie Curie (nee Sklodowska), who discovered radium in 1898.
General Kleeberg Park	NSW	Park	A park in Maitland, founded by the local Polish Association, and named after the former president of the Federal Council of Polish Associations in Australia.
Grabowsky Range	WA	Mountain range	A mountain range named after Ian Herman Grabowsky, a Scottish immigrant of Polish origin, who arrived in Australia in 1919 and became a pioneer of Australian air transport.
Gruszka Lake	WA	Lake	Named after the soldier, George Gruszka, who discovered the lake in 1961 while on a mapping mission.
Klemzig	SA	Suburb	A suburb of Adelaide, named in 1838 after the German name of a village in Poland.

Name	State/ territory	Feature	Origins
Mount Fatigue	VIC	Mountain	This peak marks one of the points on explorer Paul Strzelecki's desperate eastward march, named by his friend J Lort Stokes in the 1840s.
Mount Kosciuszko	NSW	Mountain	Australia's highest mountain was climbed and named in 1840 by the Polish explorer Paul Strzelecki, after the Polish hero Tadeusz Kosciuszko.
Mount Strzelecki	NT	Mountain	A peak north of Alice Springs in the Crawford Ranges, named in 1860 by John McDouall Stuart after the explorer Paul Strzelecki.
Odra	QLD	Street	In the town of Gailes, named after the Polish river.
Pilny	QLD	Street	In the town of Gailes, named after Pilny in Poland.
Poles Diggings	QLD	Area of land	Near Ravenswood, south of Townsville, named because it was owned by a Polish digger, Sygurd Wisniowski, who built a gold mine called 'New Warsaw'.
Polish Corner	TAS	Street corner	In Hobart, the corner of New Town and Augusta Roads on which stands the Polish–Australian brotherhood-in-arms monument.
Polish Hill River	SA	Town	Settled by Polish immigrants in the 1850s.
Polonia	QLD	Street	In the town of Gailes, the word is Polish for 'Poland'.
Swider Creek	WA	Creek	A tributary of the Carson River in the Kimberleys, named in 1954 after Frank Swider, a post-World War II Polish immigrant.
Tatra	VIC	Street	Named after Tatra, a mountain range in Poland.

Polish Names

Name	State/territory	Feature	Origins
Vistula	VIC	Street	In Melbourne, named after the Polish river.
Warsaw	VIC	Street	In Melbourne, named after the capital of Poland.

R

Radium Hill (SA)   Three times lucky?
This is probably the first place in Australia where radioactive
minerals were discovered. The town has been abandoned three
times in response to the fluctuating demand for them. It is now
a virtual ghost town.

Raworth (NSW)
Named after a place in Suffolk. (See Nostalgia, p. 151.)

Raymond Terrace (NSW)   Keen observation
This name came about in 1797 after Midshipman Raymond was
sent by boat up the Hunter River. He is said to have remarked
on the 'terraced' appearance of the trees at the junction of the
Hunter and Williams Rivers. For some time the area was known
as 'Raymond's Terraces'. (See Exploration Names, p. 66.)

Remarkable Rocks (SA)   Perched on high
A collection of boulders formed 500 million years ago, aptly
named and perched on a point in Flinders Chase National Park
on Kangaroo Island. (See Topography, p. 196.)

Research (VIC) — Keep looking

This place name is presumed to originate from a story that a lode of gold was found here, which then petered out, only to be discovered once more after a 're-search'.

Restoration Island (QLD) — Doubly restorative

Captain William Bligh landed here in 1789 after the famous mutiny on the *Bounty.* He named the island in honour of the anniversary of the restoration of King Charles II. The name, however, was doubly significant as it was applicable to the mutineers, since they were restored to health and strength on the turtle meat and palm leaf tips on the island. (See Royalty, p. 175.)

River Tamar (TAS)

Named after a river in south-western England. (See Nostalgia, p. 151.)

Robertstown (SA) — All you need is a rubber stamp

When John Roberts settled in South Australia in the 1870s, he set himself up as the first postmaster in the area in which he lived. He took the liberty of stamping letters 'Robert's Town'. This was considered by some as preferable to the colloquial name by which the area was known — Emu Flats. The post office stayed in the Roberts family until 1926, justification perhaps, if any is needed, for earning the town's name.

Rockingham (WA) — Running aground

Rockingham, 47 kilometres south of Perth, is named after the ship that in 1830 ran aground on the beach that fronts the town. It was initially salvaged but eventually sank in Cockburn Sound. (See Ship Names, p. 183.)

Roebuck Bay (WA) — Near enough is good enough

Although the bay is named after explorer William Dampier's ship, the *HMS Roebuck*, it seems fairly certain he never went there. When he came ashore, as it is thought he did in 1699, he landed further south. (See Ship Names, p. 183.)

Roleystone (WA)   Rolling along

On the outskirts of Perth, this town's name was once thought to recall 'Roleystone Manor', an estate near the birthplace of Thomas Buckingham who bought land here in 1887. However, it turns out that the district was already called 'Roleystone' before Buckingham arrived. Now it is believed more likely that it was so named because of an unusual rock formation, with a stone perched above it looking as if it was on the point of rolling down the hill. (See Topography, p. 196.)

Roma (QLD)

Roma was named after Lady Diamantina Roma Bowen, daughter of Count Roma, a Venetian nobleman. (See Royalty, p. 175.)

Roo Roo (NSW)

A homestead south of Menindee. (See Double Names, p. 101.)

Rosebery (TAS)

This is a town in north-western Tasmania. When gold was discovered here in 1893, the town sprang up, named after the British Prime Minister of the time, Archibald Rosebery.

Rosewater (SA)   A rose would smell as sweet

This suburban area 11 kilometres north-west of Adelaide was named by a local resident in an attempt to offset the smell of stagnant water from a nearby swamp. It probably didn't work.

Ross (TAS)

Named by Governor Lachlan Macquarie in 1821 after the Scottish home of one of his friends. (See Nostalgia, p. 151.)

Rottnest Island (WA)   Misty-eyed female rats

This island is generally thought to have been named by Willem de Vlamingh between 29 December 1696 and 2 January 1697 when visiting there. However, the only reference to a name in his log is 'saquen het mist eilandt', which means 'saw the island of mist'. This was later wrongly translated by a French journalist as 'Island of Girls' ('mist' was mistaken for 'miss'). The journalist believed it to be an island of an entirely female population. The present name was from a Dutch maritime clerk who interpreted Vlamingh's reference to 'wooderats' (quokkas), which inhabited the island, as rats. (See Mistakes and Apocrypha, p. 139.)

Rum Jungle (NT)   A tale of excess

Some distance to the north of Batchelor is the area known as Rum Jungle. The origin of the name is unclear, with at least three stories jostling for credibility. One argues that the area got its name because a group of wagon drivers, taking rum to the miners at Pine Creek, managed to drink 80 gallons (364 litres) of their cargo while passing through the area. Another arises from a story that a group of government officials became sidetracked, over-drank, and required a search party to make it back. A version recounted by the Northern Territory Historical Society claims that on one occasion the local hotel ran out of everything except rum, which was all that was available for the campers, one of whom remarked that it was a 'rum place' to camp. Whichever way you take it, one thing is clear: Rum Jungle acquired its name through an episode of excessive drinking of rum.

ROYALTY

The last time I recall a royal appellation being suggested for something Australian was when we changed to decimal currency on 14 February 1966. The suggestion then was to call the new unit a 'royal'. Clearly, it failed.

However, back in the times when Australia was being opened up and places were being named, respect for the monarchy was paramount. The naming of Queensland and Victoria is firmly in this tradition. But it goes well beyond this. In fact, the naming of places in Australia reflects the respect and awe of the times for those in the highest social stratum — royalty and titled aristocracy. A selection of these follows.

Place name	State	Origin
Adelaide	SA	In 1792, Prinzessin Adelheid Amalie Luise Therese Carolin was born in the castle of Meiningen, Germany. In 1818 she married the heir to the British throne and the spelling of her name changed from Adelheid to Adelaide. In 1830 William was crowned King William IV of Great Britain, and Adelaide was crowned. The capital of South Australia was named after her.
Albany	WA	A city named after Frederick, Duke of Albany and York, the favourite son of King George III.
Alberton	VIC	Named after Prince Albert, Queen Victoria's consort, in 1842. Another township on the northern boundary was named Victoria, shortly after.
Alexandrina	SA	Named after Princess Alexandrina, who later became Queen Victoria.
Augusta	WA	A town named in honour of Princess Augusta Sophia, the second daughter of King George IV and Queen Charlotte.
Brisbane	QLD	Brisbane's central business district is remarkably royalist. Some royally named streets are Anne, Adelaide, Elizabeth, Queen, Charlotte, Mary, Margaret and Alice. Running at right angles to these are George, Albert and Edward.

Place name	State	Origin
Brunswick	VIC	This suburb of Melbourne has a royal connection, although exactly to whom is in dispute. It might be in honour of Princess Caroline of Brunswick (wife of King George IV) or in honour of the marriage of Queen Victoria to Prince Albert of the royal house of Brunswick.
Clarence	WA	A townsite named after Prince William, the Duke of Clarence and Earl of Munster.
Coburg	VIC	In 1869 this area of Victoria was visited by Prince Alfred, the Duke of Saxe-Coburg. The name 'Coburg' was awarded in honour of the visit.
Franklin River	TAS	This famous, mighty river in Tasmania was named after a governor of the colony, Sir John Franklin, who arranged to have an overland track cut and surveyed from Lake St Clair to Macquarie Harbour. After its completion, in two years, the Governor and his official party completed the walk in twenty days.
Iron Baron	SA	One of a complex of iron ore mining operations including Iron Knob, Iron Monarch, Iron Princess, Iron Prince, Iron Queen, Iron Chieftain, Iron Knight and Iron Duchess.
King George Sound	WA	Named after King George III in 1791.
Nathalia	VIC	Some sources say Nathalia was the daughter of a titled European lady who gave birth in the area in the 1870s. Another version of the story is that the town is named after the Queen of Serbia, formerly Natalya Keshko, who married and had a son in the late 1870s.
Princess Royal	WA	A townsite most likely named after Victoria, Adelaide Mary Louisa, the eldest daughter of Queen Victoria.
Queens Park	WA	A suburb whose name was changed in 1911 to honour Queen Alexandra, wife of King Edward VII.
Queenscliff	VIC	Named in 1853 in honour of Queen Victoria.

Place name	State	Origin
Restoration Island	QLD	Captain William Bligh landed here in 1789 after the famous mutiny on the Bounty. He named the island in honour of the anniversary of the restoration of King Charles II.
Roma	QLD	Roma was named after Lady Diamantina Roma Bowen, daughter of Count Roma, a Venetian nobleman.
Sandringham	VIC	Named in 1888 after the royal retreat in Norfolk of the same name.
Scone	NSW	Scone was named in 1831 by a Scottish soldier who proposed that the area be called Strathearn after the Scottish valley near the Palace of Scone, the ancient crowning place of the kings of Scotland. It became the Parish of Strathearn and later the nearby village reserve became known as Scone.
Victoria Park	WA	Named after Queen Victoria.
Williamstown	VIC	Named William's Town in 1837 by Governor Richard Bourke in honour of King William IV.
Wineglass Bay	TAS	A shimmering swimming beach, named during a royal visit to Australia by Queen Elizabeth II on the yacht *Britannia*, at which time the royal party was treated to an Australian-style barbecue, including, one presumes, wine.
Yaroomba	QLD	This coastal area was first developed in 1953 when it was named Coronation Beach, in honour of Queen Elizabeth's coronation that year. It was changed in 1961 to 'Yaroomba', an Aboriginal word meaning 'surf on the beach'.

S

St A'Becket Springs (SA)   Saint or sand?

These springs in far northern South Australia were named by
Samuel Parry in 1858 after the Archbishop of Canterbury. The
name is sometimes corrupted to 'Sandy Bagot Springs'.

St Helena Island (QLD)   French imperial-style exile

The Aboriginal name for the island was 'No-gun' or 'Noogoo'. It
was a well-vegetated area valued by local indigenous people. In
1827, white settlers in the neighbouring area had some trouble
with an Aboriginal man they nicknamed 'Napoleon' because of
his apparent likeness to the French emperor. He stole an axe
from them, and by way of punishment they took him over to this
island in the bay and left him there. This proved no problem,
as he quickly made a bark canoe and paddled back to his
people on Stradbroke Island. Because Napoleon Bonaparte
had been exiled to St Helena Island in the Atlantic, the local
Europeans started calling this bay island by the same name. In
1866 prisoners were used to erect buildings on St Helena with
a view to it becoming a quarantine station, but in fact it was
turned into a prison. By 1869 over 300 prisoners lived there
in a hard-labour prison settlement. The crop grown there was

sugar cane until it was realised that this provided too many hiding places, and they planted potatoes and lucerne instead. It remained a prison until the 1930s.

St Marys Peak (SA)   Seeing through the mist
Questions surround the name of this peak sighted by E J Eyre in 1840 and named by B H Babbage in 1856. One view is that the snow on the peak of the mountain has associations with saintliness. Another view claims that there must be some mistake, as snow is a rarity on this mountain. (See Mistakes and Apocrypha, p. 139.)

Sandringham (VIC)
Named in 1888 after the Prince and Princess of Wales' house of the same name in Norfolk, England. (See Royalty, p. 175.)

Sans Souci (NSW)   Carefree
A suburb of Sydney, this French name, meaning 'without a care', was given after the Sans Souci Palace, which the Prussian King Friedrich the Great built in Potsdam in 1745. (See French Names, p. 73.)

Sarah Island (TAS)   Brutal place
This island was operated as a notorious penitentiary between 1822 and 1833. The brutal regime is described in Marcus Clarke's novel *For the Term of his Natural Life*. (See Literary Names, p. 123.)

Scone (NSW)   Devonshire tea
Scone was named in 1831 by a Scottish soldier who proposed that the area be called Strathearn after the Scottish valley near the Palace of Scone, the ancient crowning place of the kings of Scotland. It became the Parish of Strathearn and after various alterations, the nearby village reserve became known as Scone. (See Royalty, p. 175.)

Seal Rocks (NSW)   Slippery place
Named by Captain James Cook in 1770 because, when seen by

him, they were covered with seals. (See Topography, p. 196.)

Sebastopol (VIC)   Sound of guns

A town near Ballarat named after the Russian town that the British and French besieged for eleven months in 1854–55, during the battle that became the major event of the Crimean War. Apparently, the blasting of the rock for mining activity in the area was said to sound like the guns at the siege of Sebastopol. (See War Names, p. 218.)

SHEEP NAMES

The settlers who started sailing over Bass Strait from Tasmania to settle in Victoria in the 1830s were looking for sheepwalks. Spreading out over the suitably grassed areas, they established the foundation of the age of the squatter. The influence of sheep on the naming of new places is therefore not surprising. In Victoria, we find the following examples.

Place name	Location
Merino	In the Western District.
Lambing Gully	Near Seymour.
Sheep Hills	Near Warracknabeal.
Sheepwash Creek	Near Traralgon.
Sheepyard Flat	Near the Howqua River.
Woolshed	Near Beechworth.

Seven Shillings Beach (NSW)   Cheap deal

This beach is located on Sydney Harbour. Legend has it that when a Mr Busby bought a property called 'Redleaf' in 1871, an Aborigine named Gurrah had fishing rights to the beach and lived outside Redleaf's fence. Busby had trouble with Gurrah's tribe members so Mrs Busby tried to buy Gurrah's fishing rights and offered blankets, flour and clothes in exchange. Eventually,

Gurrah agreed to sell for seven shillings. The money was paid and the tribe moved on.

Sevenhill (SA)   Big plans

This area was named because when a settlement was planned here in the 1850s, it was intended that it become the evangelical and cultural centre of South Australia, rather like a small version of the city of Rome, which was built on seven hills.

Seventeen Seventy (QLD)   Fixing time

This area marks the site where Captain James Cook first landed, on 24 May 1770.

Sharksjaw Reef (TAS)   Mind that shark

This is a fang of rock poking out of the sea north of the Port Davy mouth. (See Topography, p. 196.)

Sherwood (QLD)   Green tights

A suburb of Brisbane named after the Sherwood Forest in the story of Robin Hood and his Merry Men. (See Literary Names, p. 123.)

Singleton (WA)   A good place to retire

Singleton was named after one of the region's pioneers, Francis Singleton, who came to the area in 1839 as a landed gentleman after leaving the Royal Navy. (See Nicknames, p. 146.)

Sir Edward Pellew Group (NT)   Five spices

These five islands and several rocky outcrops are located at the entrance to the McArthur River. The group was named by Matthew Flinders in honour of a distinguished officer of the British Navy.

Skillogee Creek (SA)   Thin porridge

This creek flowing through Penwortham was named by a group of surveyors who were camped on its banks. All they had to eat at the time was a thin porridge called 'skilly'.

Slacks Creek (QLD)   A fishy place
The creek that gave its name to the district was named after the Slack family, who had a cattle run there before the days of closer settlement. The Aboriginal name for it was 'Mungaree', meaning 'place of fishes', which was the name they gave to their property.

Sleeping Beauty Mountain Range (TAS)   Zzz
Part of the Wellington Range of mountains, when viewed from the Huon Valley it seems to resemble the profile of a woman sleeping on her back and so was named after the fairytale of the same name. The 'face' of the mountain is believed to resemble the hair, eyes, nose, lips, chin, neck and breast of a woman on her back. The same mountain range when seen from the Derwent Valley side is not named collectively, but has individual names for what from the south side are identified as various parts of the woman — very confusing for interstate visitors and of perhaps questionable taste from a female's perspective. (See Literary Names, p. 123.)

Snug (TAS)   Cosy fit
Believed to be derived from sailors who found 'snug' anchorage for their ships. (See Tasmanian Names, p. 199.)

Solomons Jewels (TAS)   Precious gems
This is a string of lakes named after King Solomon, son of David, who is considered the wisest of the kings of ancient Israel. (See Tasmanian Names, p. 199.)

Southern Cross (WA)   Honouring the night sky
Gold prospectors were told they should travel slightly to the east of the Southern Cross to find gold, and they did. They named the place Southern Cross. When the township was laid out, the streets were named after various constellations, for example, Altair, Antares, Sirus and Spica.

Stinky Creek (SA)   The nose speaks
Many places with unpleasant names have them changed once

the developers move in. Stinky Creek, just north of Port Lincoln, is either an exception to the general rule or has not yet been targeted by developers.

SHIP NAMES

Australia is an island as well as a continent, and a great deal of sailing — both to and around it — happened in the early history of European interest in the great southern land. The names of the ships that brought people to Australia have been a frequent resource for place naming. This is especially the case in Western Australia, as the selection below attests.

Alkimos	Named after the Greek freighter *Alkimos*.
Baldivis	The name coined by local settlers after the three ships that brought them to Western Australia — the *Balranald*, the *Diogenes* and the *Jervis Bay*.
Calista	Named after one of the first ships to bring settlers to the Swan River Colony.
Eglinton	Named after the barque *Eglinton*.
Guilderton	Named after the Dutch ship *Gilt Dragon*.
Kwinana	Taken from the wreck of the *S S Kwinana*.
Leda	Named after the brig *Leda*.
Medina	Named after the *Medina*, which arrived at the Swan River Colony in 1830.
Orelia	Orelia is named after the ship that arrived at Fremantle in 1829.
Parmelia	Named after the first ship to bring settlers to the new colony.
Rockingham	Named after a ship that ran aground in 1830.
Roebuck Bay	Named after explorer William Dampier's ship.
Success	Named after a ship commanded by Captain James Stirling.

Streaky Bay (SA) Seaweed effect

So named by Matthew Flinders who visited this area in 1802 while circumnavigating Australia. The name comes from the way the seaweed there forms long bands or streaks when subject to strong onshore winds. Local Aboriginal people call this area 'Cooeyana'. (See Topography, p. 196.)

Stroud (NSW) And then there were four

Stroud was named apparently because of the area's striking resemblance to the Cotswold countryside around the original town in England. Stroud exists on the world's map for its annual international brick-and rolling-pin throwing contest. This takes place in the Australian Stroud and contestants come from any of the four Strouds — the original, the one in Australia, and those in the United States and Canada. The first brick-throwing contest was held in 1960 between the Australian and American Strouds after it was realised that both towns had brickworks in common. In 1962, the rolling-pin contest (for women) was added. (See Nostalgia, p. 151.)

Struck Oil (QLD) Not oil at all

This town's name is derived from a play, a melodrama, of the same name. Apparently, some prospectors visiting Mount Morgan to register a claim on the Dee River saw the play and adopted the name.

Strzelecki National Park (TAS) A Pole on high

This national park located in the south-western corner of Flinders Island is named after the Polish explorer Paul Edmund de Strzelecki, who climbed its highest peak in 1842.

Strzelecki Track (SA) Polish explorer

Named for Polish-born explorer Paul Edmund de Strzelecki, who named Mount Kosciuszko. The area was pioneered by bushman and cattleduffer Harry Redford, believed to be the inspiration for Captain Starlight in Boldrewood's novel *Robbery Under Arms*. (See Exploration Names, p. 66, Literary Names, p. 123.)

Sturt Stony Desert (SA)   Dry terrain
This desolate area in north-eastern South Australia was named after the explorer Charles Sturt, who crossed it in 1845 in search of an inland sea. (See Exploration Names, p. 66.)

Subiaco (WA)   A monkish link
Subiaco's European community began to take shape in the early 1800s when Benedictine monks named it after the town in Italy where their order was founded. (See Nostalgia, p. 151.)

Success (WA)   Nothing succeeds like success
The suburb of Success is named after the ship commanded by Captain James Stirling when he visited and explored the Swan River in 1827. Apparently another name suggestion had been 'Omeo', after another ship that went aground, but because that name had already been used elsewhere, 'Success' was proposed and adopted. (See Ship Names, p. 183.)

Suggan Buggan (VIC)
The traditional Aboriginal name is 'soogin boogun', meaning 'ground'. (See Aboriginal Names, p. 11.)

Summertown (SA)   Spend your summers here
This township dates back to the 1860s when the area was known as 'New Tiers' or 'Mount Lofty'. The name 'Summertown' came into use in 1874 when a need emerged for a postal name. The local storekeeper referred to it as 'Summer Town', believing it to be an ideal place to live in during summer. By the end of the century, the name was being written as one word.

Sunday Creek (VIC)   A Sunday arrival
The explorers Hume and Hovell came upon a creek when they made their famous overland trek from Yass to Port Phillip in 1824, being the first Europeans to make this overland journey. Arriving on Sunday 12 December 1824, they named the creek, Sunday Creek, after that day. (See Special Days, p. 186.)

SPECIAL DAYS

In the early days of exploration and settlement it was not uncommon for explorers to name places for the day upon which they arrived there. For example, Captain James Cook named Whitsunday Island (QLD) when he sailed past it on Whitsunday in 1770. On Trinity Sunday, he sailed by what he named Trinity Bay, now Cairns (QLD). On occasion, Cook named places, such as Bustard Bay and Cape Tribulation in Queensland after recent events on the voyage.

In Victoria, the explorers Hume and Hovell came upon a creek when they made their famous overland trek from Yass to Port Phillip in 1824, being the first Europeans to make this overland journey. Arriving on Sunday 12 December 1824, they named the creek, Sunday Creek, after that day. In Queensland, Thursday Island is believed to have been named by Captain William Bligh, who passed by on his epic journey from Tahiti to Batavia after he had been set afloat by the mutineers from the *Bounty*.

In Tasmania, Breakfast Creek was named after a memorable breakfast. There is also Breakfast Point in NSW, near Sydney, named in 1788 with the arrival of the First Fleet. Captain John Hunter set about charting the Harbour. His records indicate that on the fifth day, he sailed west up a waterway that is now called the Parramatta River and after about 10 kilometres he put ashore to have tea and a bite to eat. This was his first charting and he named it Breakfast Point.

Birthday Siding (SA) was named because a John Bevis struck water when his stock was in need of it and it happened to be his birthday. In the last decade of the nineteenth century, the West Australian gold township of Day Dawn was named by a local gold prospector after the time of day that he pegged his claim.

Surat (QLD)   India connection

The town was surveyed in 1850 by James Burrowes and he named it after his former home town in India. The streets of Surat bear the surveyor's name and those of his family.

Swan Reach (SA)   Black swans

Situated on the Murray River, this largely pastoral area was named in honour of the many black swans that were found here when a small town sprang up after Archibald Jaffray took up the first pastoral lease in 1845.

Swansea (TAS)   Before the song

Named after Swansea in Wales by pastoralist George Meredith, Swansea was first settled in 1821 as a military post. (See Nostalgia, p. 151.)

Swider Creek (WA)   Honouring a helper

A tributary of the Carson River in the Kimberleys, this creek was named in 1954 during an expedition by the surveyor John Morgan (later Western Australia's Surveyor-General) after Frank Swider, a post-World War II Polish immigrant who assisted him during the expedition. (See Polish Names, p. 168.)

Sydney (NSW)   A penal start

European interest in the area where Sydney developed was first ignited in 1770 when it was sighted by Captain James Cook. The area surrounding Sydney Harbour, called 'Warrane' by the Aborigines, has been inhabited by the Aboriginal tribes, the Eora and the Cadigal, for at least 40000 years. The British government ordered a convict settlement to be founded by Arthur Phillip in 1788. The convicts were immediately engaged in building the settlement, which rapidly expanded. The town had streets, banks, markets and a constabulary. By 1847, convicts accounted for only 3.2 per cent of the population. Phillip named the settlement after the British Home Secretary, Thomas Townshend Sydney, 1st Viscount (1733–1801). (See Dignitaries, p. 60, Nicknames, p. 146.)

STARS

In the Brisbane suburb of McDowall, a theme of stars — in the earthly sense of famous actors — has guided the naming of streets. A selection follows.

Burlinson Close

Carides Place

Cosby Place

De Mille Street

De Vito Place

Dunaway Street

Eastwood Place

Gielgud Crescent

Goodman Close

Hackman Street

Hamilton Road

Hanks Place

Harlow Place

Ladd Close

Landon Drive

Matthau Place

Minnelli Place

Monroe Place

Neeson Crescent

Palance Crescent

Paramount Crescent

Pfeiffer Place

Pleshette Place

Redford Crescent

Seinfeld Close

Selleck Close

Sinatra Crescent

Spielberg Street

Stallone Street

Streep Place

Streisand Drive

Thurman Crescent

Ustinov Crescent

Van Dyke Crescent

In the neighbouring suburb of Bridgeman Downs, the theme of stars takes on a more celestial quality.

Apollo Place

Aquarius Place

Aries Crescent

Asteroid Place

Halleys Crescent

Lunar Place

Mercury Crescent

Orbital Close

Capricorn Place	Orion Place
Constellation Crescent	Saturn Crescent
Cosmos Place	Scorpio Place
Eclipse Street	Shuttle Place
Galaxy Street	Solar Park
Gemini Place	Voyager Crescent

T

Tally Ho (VIC) — A hunting influence

This suburb took the words of the hunting call as its name owing to the popularity of the sport in the district. The name was also widely used for various clubs and reserves.

Tanilba Bay (NSW) — The influence of war

A town near Lake Macquarie in which many streets are named by the theme of war, especially World War I, for example, Victory View, Woodrow Wilson and Avenue of the Allies. (See War Names, p. 218.)

Tarcoola (SA) — Winning by a nose

A town named after the Tarcoola goldfield, which had been named after the winner of the 1893 Melbourne Cup. (See Horses, p. 95.)

Taronga Zoo (NSW)

Named after an Aboriginal word for 'sea view'. (See Aboriginal Names, p. 11.)

Tatra (VIC)

This street in Melbourne is named after Tatra, a mountain range in Poland. (See Polish Names, p. 168.)

Temora (NSW)

Named in 1848 after a poem in *The Poems of Ossian* by James Macpherson. (See Literary Names, p. 123.)

Tempy (VIC)   Not for long

The name is believed to be a contraction of 'temporary' to show that supplies were left here temporarily for railway construction workers.

Tennyson (QLD)

This Brisbane suburb is named after the famous nineteenth-century poet, Lord Alfred Tennyson. (See Literary Names, p. 123.)

Termination Island (WA)   Farewell

So called because it was the last point seen by explorers George Vancouver and William Broughton when they sailed eastward along the southern coast in the *Discovery* and *Chatham* in 1791. (See Pessimistic Names, p. 165.)

Terrigal (NSW)   Coastal birds

Situated on the Central Coast north of Sydney, Terrigal is a popular seaside holiday destination. The first European settler in the area was John Gray, who arrived in 1826. He called his property 'Tarrygal', after the indigenous place name, a word believed to mean 'a place of little birds'.

Texas (NSW)   Disputed land

This town is situated on the Dumaresq River on the NSW–Queensland border. The area was first settled in 1842 and it was so named because, like its American namesake, the district was disputed country. Malcolm Septimus McDougall took up the land before joining his brothers on the Turon goldfields. On his return the station had been 'jumped' by another settler and it took considerable time before he was able to establish his prior claim.

The Acropolis (TAS)
This mountain was named after the citadel of Athens. (See Tasmanian Names, p. 199.)

The Blue Mountains (NSW)   Hazy origins
Popular belief has it that the Blue Mountains are so named for the blue haze that is seen from any lookout in the area and when the mountains are viewed from far away in Sydney. The technical term for this haze is the 'Rayleigh scattering', whose premise is that 'if an observer looks at a distant object with the intervening atmosphere illuminated by sunlight, the eye will receive the blue scattering rays of sunlight in addition to the rays reflected from the object itself. Therefore, any distant object will always appear to display some shade of blue' (Low 1994). In the Blue Mountains, the oil in the various species of eucalypts there evaporates in the heat of the day. It is suspended in the air, through which the sunlight passes, effectively creating a bluish tinge over the whole area.

There's another theory for the name, which is that the British naval officers who accompanied Governor Arthur Phillip and who held a number of posts in the early years of the colony, saw a similarity with the Blue Mountains of Jamaica, where most naval officers would have served at one time, as it was an important British Navy staging port in the late eighteenth century. This theory suggests that the officers would have called the area the 'Blue Mountains' as a common reference among themselves, but without officially naming the place. The name has always remained unofficial. Several formal attempts at naming failed and locals continued to use the 'Blue Mountains' as the name by which they referred to the area.

The Entrance (NSW)   Way in
A town aptly named at the opening of Tuggerah Lake to the ocean. (See Topography, p. 196.)

The Hazards (TAS)　　　　Risky business

These are solid granite mountains that rise almost sheer from the sea and are a hazard for sailors. They are named after a captain coincidentally called Albert Hazard, who lost his whaling ship *Promise* in Hazard Bay.

The Labyrinth (TAS)　　　　Mythic home

This group of lakes was named after the maze created to house the Minotaur of Greek mythology. (See Tasmanian Names, p. 199.)

The Nut (TAS)　　　　Christmas cake

The island's most northerly point is a 10 million-year-old lava plug of distinctive shape. Explorer Matthew Flinders called it 'a cliffy round lump resembling a Christmas cake'. (See Topography, p. 196.)

The Parthenon (TAS)

This mountain was named after the Greek temple in Athens. (See Tasmanian Names, p. 199.)

The Rocks (NSW)　　　　A rocky place

An area of the city of Sydney originally named because of the prevalent use of sandstone for building. It has also been noted that, given the nature of the place in the early years of settlement, many a sailor had found himself 'on the rocks' both financially and physically.

The Spectacles (WA)　　　　The eyes have it

An unusual name for this suburb of Perth, it was derived from the names of two swamps in the area, Large Eye Swamp and Small Eye Swamp. These swamps had been collectively recorded as 'The Spectacles' since 1841 when the first survey of the area was undertaken, and the suburb name was approved in 1978. Any connection with the Ophthalmia Range has not been noted. (See Ophthalmia Range, p. 149.)

The Temple (TAS)

This hill was named after the Temple in Jerusalem, which was the crowning achievement of King Solomon's reign. (See Tasmanian Names, p. 199.)

The Three Brothers (NSW)   Sibling rivalry

Captain James Cook named these hills on the mid-north coast in 1770. They were called 'brothers' because they were of comparable dimensions. Compared with their famous 'Three Sisters' in the Blue Mountains (NSW) the brothers are not well known.

The Twelve Apostles (VIC)   And then only eight

A set of stone stacks and pillars rising straight out of the sea, these were once mainland cliff fronts. The battering of the elements detached them over time from the cliff face. Lookouts from the Great Ocean Road allow the apostles (apparently there are only eight left today) to be viewed, some only visible at low tide. (See Antiquity, p. 6.)

Thirsty Sound (QLD)   Thirsty work

Named by Captain James Cook in 1770 because he and his team were unable to find fresh water there.

Thursday Island (QLD)   An island a day

This island is located at the most northern point of Queensland, at the top end of Cape York. The belief is that Captain William Bligh named it when passing by on his epic journey from Tahiti to Batavia after he had been set afloat by the mutineers from the *Bounty*. The choice of name remains mysterious; perhaps Bligh passed it on a Thursday, but it is no doubt linked to a theme of weekdays, as nearby islands are called Wednesday and Friday islands. The name started appearing in the charts in the middle of the nineteenth century. The island was settled as a government outpost in the late 1800s. An anonymous poem sums up the image of Thursday Island at the time.

Up in regions equatorial
Blessed with scenery piscatorial
Is an island known to fame.
Pearlers live and pearling thrives there,
Coloured races live in hives there,
White men only risk their lives there,
Thursday Island is its name.

(See Special Days, p. 186.)

Ti Tree (NT)　　　　　Out in the middle of nowhere

Ti Tree is a small service town in central Australia on the Stuart Highway between Alice Springs and Darwin. To the passing motorist it is not much more than a roadhouse out in the middle of nowhere. Yet, like much in this part of the world, an interesting history exists, linking the area to the Overland Telegraph Line, the problems of water in the desert, and the struggle to develop agricultural activities on marginal land. The name is pronounced (and written by some) as 'Tea Tree'. Its origin remains a mystery.

Tilla Tilla (SA)

A waterhole east of Lake Eyre. (See Double Names, p. 101.)

Tinaroo Creek (QLD)　　　　　　　　　Tin!

This creek is so called because a John Atherton is said to have cried, 'Tin, Hurroo!' when he discovered tin here.

Tom Uglys Point (NSW)　　　　　　　Poor Tom

Interpretations abound regarding the naming of Tom Uglys Point. One is that it was named after an early settler called Tom Huxley who was known as 'Huckley' by Aborigines who couldn't pronounce his name, and this then became 'Tom Ugly'. Another version claims the name derives from a man with only one leg and one arm, known as Tom Wogul or Wogully. 'Wogul' is said to mean 'one' or 'one eye' in an Aboriginal language, which was then corrupted to 'Tom Ugly'.

TOPOGRAPHY

Many place names draw their inspiration from the locality where they are found. 'Stringy Bark Creek' is exactly that — a stringy bark creek. 'Beauty Point' would likely be beautiful. This is quite a contrast with place-naming practices today, where names are sometimes given more for their marketing spin than their reflection of topographical reality, for example, Paradise Lakes or Miramar Avenue. Here is a selection of place names chosen for their topography.

Backstairs Passage (SA)

Bald Hills (QLD)

Bay of Rest (WA)

Beauty Point (TAS)

Birdsville (QLD)

Birkdale (QLD)

Black Head (NSW)

Botany Bay (NSW)

Bountiful Island (QLD)

Box Beach (NSW)

Boys Town (NSW)

Cape Upstart (QLD)

Cascade Bay (WA)

Caves Beach (NSW)

Chain of Ponds (SA)

Cherryville (SA)

Dead Heart of Australia (SA)

Devils Marbles (NT)

Dinosaur Point (SA)

Fig Tree Pocket (QLD)

Judgement Rock (TAS)

Lake Leg of Mutton (SA)

Lonesome Section (QLD)

Madmans Track (WA)

Magnetic Island (QLD)

Marble Hill (SA)

Mount Lofty (SA)

Mud Springs (QLD)

Remarkable Rocks (SA)

Roleystone (WA)

Seal Rocks (NSW)

Sharksjaw Reef (TAS)

Streaky Bay (SA)

The Coffee Pot (TAS)

The Entrance (NSW)

The Nut (TAS)

Violet Town (VIC)

Whispering Gully (NSW)

Toowoomba (QLD)

A local Aboriginal word 'tchwampa' (or 'chhwoom' or 'toowooba'), meaning 'place where melons grow' or 'water sit down'. (See Aboriginal Names, p. 11.)

Torment Point (WA)   Where's the Mortein?

Named by J Lort Stokes, the commander of the *Beagle* and the author of *Discoveries in Australia: Voyages of HMS Beagle* (Stokes 1864), because of the incessant attacks of swarms of mosquitoes. (See Pessimistic Names, p. 165.)

Toronto (NSW)   Racer's home

Named after the home city of the world champion in sculling races, Edward Hanlan, from Toronto, Canada. The championships were held in Australia in 1880. (See Nostalgia, p. 151.)

Tortilla Flats (NT)   Steinbeck's men

The locality of Tortilla Flats was named after the Government Experimental Farm in the area. The farm was given this name because it was thought the workers on the farm matched those in *Tortilla Flats*, the novel by John Steinbeck. (See Literary Names, p. 123.)

Townsville (QLD)   Magnetic town

The location of Townsville was determined by Captain Robert Towns in 1864 when he discovered a good spot adjacent to Ross River. He was a sailor and ship owner, and the place was named after him.

Trafalgar (VIC)   Nelson's win

Located 124 kilometres south-east of Melbourne in rich dairy and agricultural country, Trafalgar was first settled in the 1860s and named after the famous naval battle in which the British, led by Nelson, defeated the French and Spanish fleets. (See War Names, p. 218.)

Transvaal Square (VIC)   Boer gun

This reserve in Geelong, in which an ancient muzzle-loading gun was placed, was created to commemorate the Boer War of 1899–1902. (See War Names, p. 218.)

Trundle (NSW)

Trundle was named after a suburb of outer London. (See Nostalgia, p. 151.)

Tucki Tucki (NSW)

A state forest south of Lismore. (See Double Names, p. 101.)

Tumble Down Dick (NSW)   Falling over drunk

The story is that the name commemorates a blind horse that fell down a hillside to its death while leading a bullock team. But rather more likely is that it originates from 'Tumbledown Dick', a popular name for English pubs, said to be an uncomplimentary reference to Oliver Cromwell's drunken son. (See Horses, p. 95.)

Tumby Bay (SA)   Thinking of home

Named by explorer Matthew Flinders after a parish of his native Lincolnshire in England.

TASMANIAN NAMES

According to those promoting Tasmania as a tourist destination, one of the many good reasons to visit it is the plethora of unusual place names. These can be grouped thematically — as the selection below suggests.

Theme	Examples
Cute, affectionate names	Beauty Point, Bell Bay, Daisy Bell, Fern Tree, Flowerdale, Flowerpot, Flowery Gully, Golden Valley, Grassy, Hideaway Bay, Kindred, Nook, Oyster Cove, Paradise, Pearshape, Primrose Sands, Quamby Brook, Retreat, Rosegarland, Rosevale, Snug, Sunnyside, Tea Tree, The Gardens and The Glen.
Bizarre or ignominious names	Back Creek, Cramps, Detention River, Electrona, Falmouth, Needles, Police Point, Sandfly, Smokers Bank, Squeaking Point, Tinderbox and Tunnel.
Quirky names	Catamaran, Christmas Hills, Cooee, Crabtree, Cuckoo, Diddledum Plains, Doo Town, Dromedary, Egg and Bacon Bay, Egg Lagoon, English Town, Figure of Eight Creek, Irishtown, Jetsonville, Meander, Milkshake Hills, Nowhere Else, Ouse, Penguin, Penzance, Plenty, Quoiba, Redpa, Sea Elephant, Steppes, The Banca and Tomahawk.

Biblical and mythological names

There is a story about an explorer-soldier called Hugh Germain who, in 1804–09, accompanied by two convicts, explored the hinterland of Hobart, shooting kangaroos to feed the settlement. Germain was reputed to have two books with him, the Bible and The Arabian Nights and these constant companions suggested the names of places around Hobart such as Jericho, Jerusalem, River Jordan, Lake Tiberius and Bagdad. In this way, too, a collection of pretty lakes on the

Central Plateau became Solomons Jewels, some rocky crags became the Walls of Jerusalem, a giant stone monolith became King Davids Peak, and a placid lake became Lake Salome.

However, a closer look tells us that more sources of inspiration were called on, though they, too, were largely drawn from classical mythology, as Harry Loots (1998) described in the narrative of a bushwalk he took with his companion, Lindy.

'We crossed a land called the Lake Country. It has over 4000 lakes ... We followed tracks and camped at spots that have been well patronised by bushwalkers since the 1930s. They celebrated this other world, the reflections on its lakes, the cube shaped bluestone on its bare mountains and the ancient pencil pines that grow among velvety green cushion plants in this alpine environment with names of another world. Place names were borrowed from ancient history. We walked from the Biblical names of the Old Testament into the world of the gods of Classical Greece.'

The following are some of the place names he discovered along the way.

Name type	Name	Geographical feature	Origin
Biblical names	Damascus Gate	Pass	The main gate into the old city of Jerusalem.
	Ephraims Gate	Pass	The northern gate into the old city of Jerusalem — Ephraim was the younger son of Jacob.

Name type	Name	Geographical feature	Origin
	Herods Gate	Pass	A north-facing gate in the old city of Jerusalem, so named because it led to the place where King Herod's palace used to be. Herod was a ruler of ancient Galilee and is best known for his role in the execution of Jesus.
	King Davids Peak	Bluestone mountain	David ruled for forty years as king of ancient Israel.
	Lake Salome	Lake	Salome was the mother of Jesus' apostles, James and John.
	Lake Sidon	Lake	An important city in ancient Phoenicia criticised in the Old Testament as being a place of idolatry and materialism.
	Pool of Bethesda	Body of water	The biblical Pool of Bethesda (meaning 'house of mercy') was considered a place of healing.
	Pool of Siloam	Body of water	The Pool of Siloam (meaning 'sent') was a huge basin at the lowest point in the city of Jerusalem.
	Solomons Jewels	String of lakes	King Solomon, son of David, is considered the wisest of the kings of ancient Israel.
	The Temple	Hill	The Temple in Jerusalem was the crowning achievement of King Solomon's reign.

Tasmanian Names

Name type	Name	Geographical feature	Origin
	Walls of Jerusalem	Mountain	Refers to the walls that enclosed the old city of Jerusalem, pierced by eight gates.
	Zion Gate	Pass	'Zion', from Hebrew, refers to a fortress hill within Jerusalem, and became symbolic of the entire city. The Zion Gate is the southern entrance to the Old City of Jerusalem.
	Zion Hill	Hill	
	Zion Vale	Valley	
Greek mythological names	Cephissus	Creek and waterfalls	River god.
	Cynthia Bay	Bay	Goddess of the moon.
	Lake Ophion	Lake	Named after a huge mythological serpent.
	Mount Olympus	Mountain	Home of the supreme Greek gods.
	Mount Ossa	Mountain	Ossa was the goddess of rumour. There is also a Greek mountain of the same name.
	Narcissus River	River	A beautiful youth who fell in love with his own image.
	Pelion Gap	Mountain	Home of the centaurs.
	The Acropolis	Mountain	The citadel of Athens.

Name type	Name	Geographical feature	Origin
	The Labyrinth	Lakes	A maze created to house the Minotaur.
	The Parthenon	Mountain	The Greek temple in Athens.
Norse mythological names	Lake Thor	Lake	The Scandinavian god of war.
Miscellaneous names	Gate of the Chain	Pass	A part of the old city of Jerusalem that serves as the entrance to the Temple Mount, leading to the Dome of the Rock and the El Aksa Mosque.
	Jaffa Vale	Valley	Jaffa is a coastal town that was the historic port to ancient Israel.
	Lake Petrarch	Lake	An Italian Renaissance poet.

U

Ulladulla (NSW)   Holy harbour

A town on the south-eastern coast of NSW, on Dhurga Aboriginal land, it was once known as 'Holy Dollar', which was thought to be a corruption of the Aboriginal name 'Woolladoorh', meaning 'safe harbour'. More recently, however, doubt has been cast on the origins of the name.

Ultimo (NSW)   Lucky month

Ultimo owes its name to an incident in 1803. Apparently, John Harris, a surgeon who had fallen foul of the Rum Corps, was due to be court marshalled. He beat the charges when it was discovered the court papers had incorrectly recorded the date of his supposed offence as 'ultimo', meaning 'last month' instead of 'instant', meaning 'of this month'. Harris subsequently named his house 'Ultimo' to commemorate the incident. The area became known by the name of the house.

Uluru (NT)   Sacred rock

This massive rock in central Australia was formerly known as 'Ayers Rock' but it is now known by its traditional Aboriginal name, 'Uluru'. The former name was given in 1873 to honour

Sir Henry Ayers, the Chief Secretary of South Australia at the time. The rock rises 348 metres above the plain and is about 9 kilometres around the base. The area is home to two groups of Western Desert people — the Yankunytjatjara and the Pitjantjatjara. In 1985, the rock was handed back to the traditional owners, the Anangu people. Uluru is a sacred place, its physical features having special significance to the local indigenous people. (See Changed Names, p. 30.)

Ulverstone (TAS)   On the banks of the Leven
This town west of Launceston is situated on the banks of the Leven River and is the centre of a farming and agricultural district. It was first settled around 1848 and was slow to develop. In its early days it was known as 'The Leven', after the river on which it is located. Details of how the name 'Ulverstone' came to be are not known but it is thought to be named after a place in England.

Undara (QLD)   The past in the present
This place in the bushland south-west of Cairns, is famous for its lava tubes, reputed to be the largest in the world. It is reached by guided tour only and managed by people involved closely with eco-tourism. 'Undara' is an Aboriginal word meaning 'a long way'.

Undera (VIC)
This name is derived from an Aboriginal word meaning 'fat'. (See Aboriginal Names, p. 11.)

Uraidla (SA)   Ears in the sky
Opinion has it that this name derives from the Kaurna word 'yurreidla', meaning 'two ears', which it is believed refers to the similarity of two nearby mountains, Lofty and Bonython. Especially when viewed against the western skyline, they seem to resemble the ears of a giant kangaroo that exists as a creature in Kaurna lore.

Uralla (NSW)   Meaning unknown

This place is situated between Armidale and Tamworth and its name remains a matter of conjecture. It may be derived from a local indigenous word meaning 'at the camp'. Other suggestions for its meaning are 'big hill', 'open running water' and 'high mountain'.

Urana (NSW)   Look up and listen

This town gets its name, it is believed, from a local indigenous word meaning 'the noise of flying quail'.

Urbenville (NSW)   No city in this country

This place name is an example of how names given to places can mislead. The 'urban' in this name seems to suggest a link to a city, perhaps on the outskirts, but in fact, as the travel literature puts it, 'there is nothing urban about this NSW–Queensland border town perched high on a Richmond Range plateau with views that go on forever'.

Vanderlin Island (NT)   Mistaken identity
The largest of the islands in the Sir Edward Pellew Group, it was originally named 'Cape Vanderlin' and thought to have been named by Abel Tasman in 1644 when he mistakenly mistook it for a part of the mainland.

Varroville (NSW)   Ancient agriculture
Varroville was the name given by Dr Robert Townson to a grant of land near Minto, near Campbelltown. It was named after Marcus Terentius Varro, an ancient Roman writer, of whose books only three on agriculture and stock farming survive.

Vaucluse (NSW)
This harbourside Sydney suburb was first called 'Valla Clausa', meaning an 'enclosed valley'. The Aboriginal name was said to be 'Kulong'.

Vault Point (NSW)   Locked in
The rather odd name derives from the fact that the Rodd family owned a vault on the point.

Venus Bay (VIC)   Women are from Venus

The French called this 'Baie de la Venus', after the ship *Venus* in which George Bass sailed to the Pacific Islands to buy supplies for his settlement in Sydney. (See French Names, p. 73.)

Venus Tor (NSW)   Named by two women

This 'butte', or isolated hill rising abruptly above the surrounding land, was named 'Venus Beacon Tor' in 1935 by conservationists Marie Beuzeville Byles and Marjorie Shaw. The 'Beacon' was later dropped, as 'tor' is the correct name for this geological feature.

Verdun (SA)   Blood-soaked battle

One of the German-populated towns of the Adelaide Hills that had its name changed during World War I, in this case to commemorate one of the bloodiest battles of that war. (See War Names, p. 218.)

Veterans Flat (NSW)   A long way from Europe

This locality near Maitland is named in memory of about a dozen veterans of the Napoleonic wars who settled in the area between 1829 and 1831.

Victor Brazier Park (NSW)   A son remembers

This is a reserve in South Granville. Victor Brazier was the owner of a farm on this site, which he bought in 1946–47. He served in the RAN for twenty-five years, including during World War II when he was one of only thirteen survivors of the *HMAS Yarra*, sunk by the Japanese in Sundra Strait, Indonesia. The name was suggested by Victor's son, Norman Brazier, in response to the council's 1997 invitation to name 104 unnamed parks and reserves.

Victoria Park (WA)

Named after Queen Victoria. (See Royalty, p. 175.)

Villawood (NSW)   Inverted letters

This suburb near Fairfield takes its name from its railway

station, which was named 'Woodville Road' when it opened in 1922, being named after a road running through the suburb. However, because of some confusion with another Woodville, the name was transposed to create 'Villawood'.

Vinces Hill (NSW)   Early seachanger

Located in the Bathurst region, this hill was named after Vincent Murnane, an early settler who took up a conditional purchase on a number of lots. He built a hut and lived on the bank of a local creek in one of them.

Vinegar Hill (NSW)   Early Eureka

The name 'Vinegar Hill' has a deeply textured history of enduring significance to Irish Australians. In March 1804, approximately one-third of the European population of Sydney comprised Irish political prisoners, many of whom had been sent to the colony following their failed political uprising at the Battle of Vinegar Hill in Wexford County, Ireland, some six years earlier. Many others had been killed or executed in that battle. In the Australian plot, the plan was to raise a rebel army of one thousand Irishmen, raised from a number of sites around Sydney, and to march on Sydney, take ships from the harbour, and sail for freedom. They were motivated by a desire to live in an Ireland free of English occupation. However, the coordination of the revolt went awry and it failed. The story of the attempted rebellion was suppressed in the early nineteenth century to avoid encouraging similar insubordination to British rule in the colony. As a result, it is not as well known as the story of the Eureka Stockade some fifty years later. The name 'Vinegar Hill' was used as the password for entry to the Eureka Stockade.

Violet Town (VIC)   Wild colour

This is a pretty township 170 kilometres north-east of Melbourne. The first known European in the vicinity was Major Thomas Mitchell who, in 1836, camped by some ponds where wild violets were in flower. He named the spot 'Violet Ponds', which later became 'Violet Town'. (See Topography, p. 196.)

Vistula (VIC)

In Melbourne, this street is named after the Polish river. (See Polish Names, p. 168.)

Vivonne Bay (SA)

Named after Louis Victor de Rochechouart, Duc de Mortemart et de Vivonne. (See French Names, p. 73.)

Volkers Park (NSW)   Big trees start as seeds

This park in Grafton is named after a seed merchant who planted the first jacaranda trees in the early 1870s, for which the area later became famous.

Von Guerard Park (NSW)   Golden landscapes

Named in honour of Eugene von Guerard, who is widely regarded as Australia's most important landscape artist of the 1850s and 1860s. He came to Australia in 1852 to join the gold rush and was based in Melbourne. His painting, *Sydney Heads*, is regarded by many as the quintessential image of Sydney.

Voyager Memorial Park (NSW)   Tragic voyage

Located near Huskisson, this park commemorates a tragic accident when *HMAS Voyager* sank after a collision with *HMAS Melbourne* during night exercises off Jervis Bay, in February 1964, with a loss of eighty-two lives.

W

Waddamana Power Station (TAS)   Big noisy river

Waddamana is derived from the Aboriginal word meaning 'big river' or 'noisy water'. It is the site of the first of Tasmania's twenty-seven power stations and operated commercially between 1916 and 1965.

Wadderin (WA)

Located in the central agricultural region of the state, the name derives from the Aboriginal name of a nearby hill, first recorded in 1865. The word is similar to another one meaning 'doe kangaroo'. (See Aboriginal Names, p. 11.)

Wagga Wagga (NSW)   Black bird

A large regional centre on the banks of the Murrumbidgee River in the Riverina district of southern NSW, it is thought that the name derives from the Aboriginal word for 'crow'. The repetition provides emphasis implying there were many crows in the area. (See Double Names, p. 101.)

Wahroonga (NSW)

Named after an Aboriginal word meaning 'our home'. (See Aboriginal Names, p. 11.)

Wakefield (NSW)

Named after Wakefield, Yorkshire. (See Nostalgia, p. 151.)

Walhalla (VIC)   Forever and ever

A gold-mining town located about 170 kilometres east of Melbourne, it was originally called Stringers Creek after the waterway of the same name that runs through the ravine. It changed its name to Walhalla in 1869. The present name would seem to derive from Valhalla, the hall of immortality in Norse mythology where heroes reside after being slain in battle. (See Antiquity, p. 6.)

Walla Walla (VIC)

A creek near Warragul. (See Double Names, p. 101.)

Walls of Jerusalem (TAS)

This mountain was named after the walls that enclosed the old city of Jerusalem, pierced by eight gates. (See Tasmanian Names, p. 199.)

Wangi Wangi (NSW)   Night-time residents

This small community on the shores of Lake Macquarie takes its name from the local Aboriginal word meaning 'many night owls'.

Warrandyte (VIC)   Bullseye

A combination of the Aboriginal words 'warran', meaning 'to throw', and 'dyte', meaning 'the object aimed at'. (See Aboriginal Names, p. 11.)

Warrawarrapiralilullamalulacoupalynya (NT)

This place name, whose meaning is unknown, was collected by Reverend John Flynn of the Australian Inland Mission in the 1930s, and was said to be the longest in Australia. However, the Northern Territory Department of Lands can find no evidence of the existence of a place with this name. According to the *South Australian Gazetteer*, the longest official name in Australia is 'Mamungkukumpurangkuntjunya Hill' in outback

South Australia (p. 128). See also Lake Caddiwarrabirracanna (SA), p. 115.

Warsaw (VIC)

In Melbourne, this street is named after the capital of Poland. (See Polish Names, p. 168.)

Warwick (QLD)   Social protest

The town of Warwick on the Darling Downs is not, as is commonly thought, named after the English city of Warwick. Rather, it was named after a character in a novel — Warwick the Kingmaker in Lord Lytton's *The Last of the Barons,* published in 1843. In the book, the character Warwick fought against the tide of social change that saw the English barons losing their power. Presumably, when squatters Patrick and George Leslie were asked to suggest a name for the village being planned on part of their principality, the character of Warwick must have had a special significance. (See Literary Names, p. 123.)

Watanobbi Knoll (NSW)   Careful what you say

Apparently, this name was born when a local Central Coast farmer was talking about his property one day and remarked that it was 'a knobby piece of land'. The name stuck.

Waverley (VIC)

A city in Victoria named by an early settler after Sir Walter Scott's *'Waverley'* novels. (See Literary Names, p. 123.)

Wayatinah (TAS)   The power of a tiny creek

This small village takes its name from the local Aboriginal word that means 'creek'. These days it is home to people connected to the Hydro-Electric Scheme and is part of the larger network of power stations.

Weipa (QLD)   Hunting for God in bauxite country

Located on the Gulf of Carpentaria, the town was originally established as a Presbyterian mission in 1898. The discovery of bauxite followed several years later. The name comes from a local Aboriginal word thought to mean 'hunting ground'.

Welcome Hill (TAS)   Gratitude

In 1827, an expedition of new settlers encountered bad weather and ran out of food and water. When finally they sighted the sea from this hill, the name was bestowed in thankful relief.

Welcome Hill (WA)   Sight for sore eyes

In 1863, on the West Australian side of the continent, the words, 'It's a welcome sight!' were apparently exclaimed by the wife of John Withell, when shown the camping place for the night. These pioneer settlers were on their way from Cossack to Roebourne, and the journey and exclamation resulted in the hill's naming.

Wellesley (SA)

A point near Elliston named in honour of the Duke of Wellington, whose name was Arthur Wellesley. (See War Names, p. 218.)

Wellington (SA)

A town near Lake Alexandrina named after the Duke of Wellington, the hero of the Battle of Waterloo. (See War Names, p. 218.)

West End (QLD)   Local version

This Brisbane suburb was named by the English settlers after the famous West End of London. (See Nostalgia, p. 151.)

Western Port (VIC)   West is east

The best description of the naming of this place is found in the writings of the late Chris Richards. 'Sometimes, even simple names can present a puzzle. To the west of Melbourne we have the Western District, while to the east we have Western Port? How can the west be in the east? The answer is simple if you follow the progress of settlement in Victoria. When the explorer George Bass sailed into Bass Strait in 1798 Victoria had not yet been settled by Europeans. Bass had sailed from Sydney and reached a position on the south-west coast of New South

Wales, which then included Victoria. Bass wrote in his journal that, "I have named the place, from its relative situation to every other known harbour on the coast, Western Port." By way of contrast the Western District was named after the European settlement of Victoria had commenced in 1834–35. This name reflected its relative position within the District of Port Phillip, which became the state of Victoria. So sometimes, "east is west and west is west, and never the twain shall meet!"' (Richards, personal correspondence, undated).

Whispering Gully (NSW)   Rumours

The early prospectors and woodcutters reported hearing whisperings in the gully. (See Topography, p. 196.)

Whitsunday Island (QLD)

Captain James Cook named this island when he sailed past it on Whitsunday in 1770. (See Special Days, p. 186.)

Who'da Thought it Hill (NSW)   Surprise, surprise

The views from the lookout atop this hill is such that might explain its name. Local legend claims that the name comes from the surprise felt by travellers upon encountering the spectacular view from the top.

Wickham (WA)   Beagle boy

Wickham takes its name from Captain John Wickham who explored the area aboard the *HMS Beagle* in 1838.

Wilberforce (NSW)

Named after William Wilberforce, eighteenth-century anti-slavery campaigner. (See Dignitaries, p. 60.)

Williamstown (SA)   Land for horse

A local legend says the land in this area was traded to a Scot for a mob of horses. It was then subdivided for settlement and named after the owner's eldest son. (See Horses, p. 95.)

Williamstown (VIC)

Named William's Town in 1837 by Governor Richard Bourke in honour of the king of the time, King William IV. (See Royalty, p. 175.)

Wilmington (SA)   American cousin

Once known as 'Beautiful Valley' because of the scenic southern Flinders Ranges, it was named Wilmington in 1876 when the governor of the time, Sir Anthony Musgrave, named it thus because his wife had an association with a town of the same name in the state of Delaware in the United States.

Winchelsea (VIC)   Breeding like rabbits

First known as 'Barwon', this place developed mainly because of its reputation as a handy ford on the Barwon River. In 1851, it was renamed 'Winchelsea' by Governor La Trobe. One of the first residents of the area was a successful grazier named Thomas Austin who arrived in 1837. Austin is credited (perhaps 'blamed' is the better term) for the introduction of rabbits into Australia, as he released twelve pairs into the wild for the purposes of hunting. By 1865, 20000 rabbits had been shot but this did little to stem the tide.

Windjana Gorge National park (WA) Guerrilla tactics

The gorge itself was cut millions of years ago by the Lennard River as it ran through the Napier Range. In the 1890s an Aboriginal police tracker named Jandamarra mounted a guerrilla campaign against whites in order to stem their encroachment into the area. The national park takes its name from the Wandjina spirits, whom the local Burumba people believed visited the area during the Dreamtime.

Windorah (QLD)   Bogged down

Originally known as Stony Point, the place now named Windorah is thought to be an Aboriginal name that means 'place of large fish' in reference to the waterholes of nearby Cooper Creek. The exact site of the town was decided by the fact that a bullock wagon loaded with stores became hopelessly bogged here. Anybody who wanted stores had to come to this spot. As a result, a series of shanty dwellings sprang up in the area.

Windsor (NSW)

Named after the royal town of Windsor on the Thames, England. (See Nostalgia, p. 151.)

Wineglass Bay (TAS)   Under the influence

A shimmering swimming beach, named during a royal visit to Australia by Queen Elizabeth II on the yacht *Britannia*, at which time the royal party was treated to an Australian-style barbecue, including, one presumes, wine. (See Royalty, p. 175.)

Winnelli (NT)   Two women are better than one

Derived from the name of an army camp, which itself was derived from joining together 'Winifred' and 'Nellie', the names of the wives of two officers who were involved in building the camp.

Wollongong (NSW)   Hard ground near water

Many different meanings have been suggested for this place name, derived from a local Aboriginal word. Some of these are 'song' or 'sound of the sea or waves', 'wedding feast', 'hard ground near water', 'five clouds' or 'five islands'. Another claim, unlikely and unverified, is that the word means 'See the monster comes', as an expression of fear by Aborigines as they saw for the first time an approaching ship in full sail. (See Nicknames, p. 146.)

Wolseley (SA)

A town north of Naracoorte named after Sir Garnet Joseph Wolseley, a hero of Britain's Egyptian wars of the 1880s. (See War Names, p. 218.)

Wongle Wongle (QLD)

This is a creek north-west of Goondiwindi. (See Double Names, p. 101.)

Woodend (VIC)   Out in the open

A sleepy town some 70 kilometres north-west of Melbourne at an elevation of 560 metres, the town is located near Hanging Rock, which is famous from Joan Lindsay's novel *Picnic at Hanging Rock*. The book was made into a very successful film. Woodend was named literally because it was the end of the wood — where in the mid-nineteenth century, gold prospectors, heading north to the goldfields around Bendigo, could feel that they were out of the reach of bushrangers who hid in the woodlands waiting to prey on them. A township emerged to cater to the passing trade. (See Literary Names, p. 123.)

Woy Woy (NSW)

A town on the Central Coast. (See Double Names, p. 101.)

WAR NAMES

When soldiers return from wars, an accepted way by which a nation shows its gratitude is to remember their feats and sacrifices by naming places after theatres of war. With no shortage of wars in which Australians have served and fallen, a strong military theme can be seen in the naming of places over the last two hundred years of Australian history. A selection is listed below.

Name	State/ territory	Geographical feature
Anzac Hill	NT	A hill in Alice Springs.
Attack Creek	NT	A creek north of Tennant Creek.
Bapaume	QLD	A township near Stanthorpe.
Bay of Waterloo	SA	A bay on the west coast of South Australia.
Birdwood	SA	A town in the Torrens Valley.
Bugaldie	NSW	A town north of Gilgandra.
Cannon Hill	QLD	A suburb of Brisbane.

Name	State/ territory	Geographical feature
Cape Duquesne	VIC	A cape near Portland.
Fairmile Cove	NSW	A cove in the Parramatta River.
Hill Sixty	NSW	A hill near Inverell.
Holbrook	NSW	A town near Albury.
Holdsworth Avenue	NSW	A street in Muswellbrook.
Jack Jewry Reserve	NSW	A public reserve in St Marys.
Kitchener	NSW	A town near Cessnock.
Lemnos	NSW	A street in the suburb of Cooks Hill.
Lenswood	SA	A town in the Adelaide Hills.
Lock	SA	A small country community.
Messines	QLD	A town near Stanthorpe.
Mount Spion Kopje	VIC	A mountain near Myrtleford.
Nelson Bay	NSW	A town in Port Stephens.
Picton	NSW	A town south of Campbelltown.
Prevelly	WA	A township near Augusta.
Sebastopol	VIC	A town near Ballarat.
Tanilba Bay	NSW	A town near Lake Macquarie.
Trafalgar	VIC	A town south-east of Melbourne.
Transvaal Square	VIC	A reserve in Geelong.
Verdun	SA	A town in the Adelaide Hills.
Wellesley	SA	A point near Elliston.
Wellington	SA	A town near Lake Alexandrina.
Wolseley	SA	A town north of Naracoorte.
Yea	VIC	A small rural centre in north-eastern Victoria.

X

Xantippe (WA)   Mysterious shrew

A rural locality north-east of Perth, the area takes its name from antiquity. Xanthippe was a late fifth-century BC Athenian matron, the wife of Socrates, and mother of his three sons. Legend suggests that she was somewhat of a shrew, for her name became synonymous with a nagging wife. But why this district in Western Australia should be so named remains a mystery.

Y

Yackandandah (VIC)
This is the traditional Aboriginal name, derived from the word 'tackan', meaning 'something extraordinary'. (See Aboriginal Names, p. 11.)

Yangilluo (WA)   You could do worse
One, perhaps romantic, interpretation of this place name, is that it was the local Aboriginal word for 'place of love'.

Yantabulla (NSW)   Stony spring
Located near Bourke, the name comes from the Aboriginal word meaning 'stones around a spring'. The place was named after Vincent Dowling's homestead called 'Yantabulla-Bulla', which was later the site of the Yantabulla Hotel.

Yaroomba (QLD)   Queen dumped by the beach
This coastal area was first developed in 1953 when it was named Coronation Beach, in honour of Queen Elizabeth's coronation that year. It was changed in 1961 to Yaroomba, an Aboriginal word meaning 'surf on the beach'. (See Changed Names, p. 30, Royalty, p. 175.)

Yarra River (VIC)   Misunderstood

The river was originally named 'Freshwater River' by early European surveyors in 1803. It is claimed to have been renamed subsequently by a surveyor named John Wedge in 1835. He apparently asked some local Aborigines what they called the lower reaches of the river. He mistook their reply of 'Yarro Yarro', meaning 'it flows', for 'Yarra Yarra'.

Yarramundi (NSW)   Healer of pain

The name is connected to an Aboriginal healer, who operated on one of Governor Arthur Phillip's guides who was suffering pain.

Yarranbah (NSW)   Comfort stop

Yarranbah was the site of a Cobb and Co coach station, which supplied meals and accommodation as well as fresh horses for travellers and coaches. The name is Aboriginal but no recorded meaning for it exists.

Yass (NSW)   Yes, please

The story goes that in the 1820s, the explorer Hamilton Hume sent a man out to evaluate the country beyond. When he returned, Hume asked him if there was good country ahead. He replied 'Ya-ass-plains'. Hume was tickled by this and adopted the name 'Yass Plains' for the district that came to be known as Yass. Another version of this story has it that the name comes from an Aborigine's comments to Hume, 'Yass boss, plains'. Others say this is folk myth, maintaining that the name of 'Yass' is a corruption of native words.

Yaven Yaven (NSW)

A creek near Wagga Wagga. (See Double Names, p. 101.)

Yea (VIC)   Is that a yes?

Yea is a small rural centre in north-eastern Victoria. It was surveyed in 1856 and named after a Colonel Lacy Yea who was killed in the Crimean War. (See War Names, p. 218.)

Yeagerton (NSW)   A steamy, eager young American
This name comes from William Tudor Yeagerton, a young emigrant from the United States, who ran steamers on the Richmond River where he eventually established a steamer monopoly.

Yellow Womans Gully (NSW)   Mysterious colour
The name originated in the first half of the nineteenth century, after a shepherd who lived and worked locally. The name was also used for a nearby creek. But why the shepherd was known as the 'yellow woman' remains a mystery.

Yerin Creek (NSW)   A local called Yerin
This creek is located near Gosford and was named after a local Darkinjung member who worked for the Forestry Department and was killed at work. He was called 'Yerin' by the Europeans with whom he worked.

Yes I Know Rock (NSW)   But what did he know?
This rocky outcrop near Forster reputedly owes its name to an incident that occurred during big seas. Apparently, these were the last words of a fisherman who was washed from this rock. His fate is unknown.

Yetman (NSW)   Lost in a squatting history
A village on the Macintyre River near Inverell, it was originally the name of a squatting run held in 1848 by a squatter named Dight. It is now believed that the word comes from the Bigumbil language, but no meaning has been recorded.

Yorkeys Knob (QLD)   Living on the beach
Named after a local fisherman called 'Yorkey' who lived on the rocky hill ('knob') adjacent to Half Moon Beach in the 1880s. He was believed to have come from Yorkshire in England. (See Nicknames, p. 146.)

Yorky Gully (NSW)   Track clearer leaves his name
In the early 1900s, a pioneer timber cutter, Yorky Waters, cleared the track, which is south of this gully and runs parallel to it. He

was remembered long after through the place name.

You Yangs (VIC)

This name comes from the Aboriginal words 'wurdi youang' or 'ude youang', meaning 'big mountain in the middle of a plain'. (See Aboriginal Names, p. 11.)

Young Gully (NSW)   Pioneering spirit

Named after a community-minded carpenter called Harry Young who in the 1940s was the first person to clear and farm the land next to this gully. The Youngs were a well-known pioneering family in the district.

Yowie Bay (NSW)   Lamb chops

In this little bay in Port Hacking, sheep were bred by Thomas Holt in the nineteenth century. Holt employed shepherds from Yorkshire, England, and since 'yowie' is a Yorkshire word for 'lamb', this would seem to be the most plausible explanation for the name.

Yulara (NT)   Hospitality spot

This town was started in 1984 for the sole purpose of catering to the needs of visitors to Uluru and the surrounds, some 20 kilometres away. The name Yulara is an Aboriginal word that means 'place of the howling dingo'.

Yuleba (QLD)   Blue waterlilies

This town took the name of the old Yuleba homestead from which the town sprang. The word is thought to mean 'the place of blue waterlilies'.

Yurulbin (NSW)   Too nosey by far

This is a point situated at the most northern tip of Snails Bay, where the Lane Cove and Parramatta Rivers meet to form Sydney Harbour. The Aboriginal name, 'Yerroulbin', meaning 'swift running water', was given to the point after a request from the local council in 1992 suggested the name be changed from 'Long Nose Point'.

Z

Zeehan (TAS)　　　　　　　　　Shipping names
Mount Zeehan and the western coastal settlement of Zeehan were both named after one of the two ships in Abel Tasman's 1642 expedition.

Zeldaline Gardens (NSW)　　　　　Good neighbour
This little park in Rooty Hill was named after Zeldaline Marjorie Smith, who died in 2000 after being a long-time active member of community, residents' and environmental groups.

Zetland (NSW)　　　　　　The weight of an earl
A suburb of Sydney named in the 1870s after the Earl of Zetland, a relative of the governor of the time, Sir Hercules Robinson.

Zig Zag Creek (NSW)　　　　　　Railway creek
This creek was named after the Thornleigh Zig Zag Railway, which was situated in the same area as the creek. The railway was constructed by Amos and Company for the purpose of obtaining ballast for their new construction work. It provided access to a quarry, which was 1.2 kilometres from the site of Thornleigh Station and about 30 metres below it. The name was proposed by Lee Macquarie Smith, a student at Normanhurst

High School, as part of the Berowra Catchment Management Committee's creek-naming competition.

Zion Gate (TAS)   Enter the fortress

This is the name of a pass. 'Zion', from Hebrew, refers to a fortress hill within Jerusalem, and became symbolic of the entire city. The Zion Gate is the southern entrance to the Old City of Jerusalem. (See Tasmanian Names, p. 199.)

Zuytdorp Cliffs (WA)   Lost relics

Named after the Dutch ship *Zuytdorp*, which has lain at the base of the cliffs from the time it was wrecked there en route from Holland to the East Indies in 1712. The origin of the ship was not known until the 1950s when research into some relics found by a local stockman were identified as belonging to the *Zuytdorp*. It is known that some survivors made it to shore but their ultimate fate is a mystery.

References

Every effort has been made to include all sources consulted during the research for this book. Should any omissions be found, please contact the publisher so that amendments can be made to subsequent editions.

Appleton, R & B 1992, *The Cambridge Dictionary of Australian Place Names*, Cambridge University Press, Melbourne, p. x.

Arthur, JM 2003, *The Default Country: A Lexical Cartography of Twentieth-century Australia*, University of NSW Press, Sydney, p. 72.

Bishop, G 2005, 'East Torrens placenames and local history', *Placenames Australia*, June, pp. 8–9.

Blair, D 2004, 'Naming places and placing names', *Placenames Australia*, March, pp. 10–11.

Bloomfield, N 2004, 'French Names in Australia', *Placenames Australia*, December, pp. 4–5.

Bonyhady T & Griffiths T (eds.) 2002, *Words for Country: Landscape and Language in Australia*, University of NSW Press, Sydney.

Cannon, J 2004, 'Unusual and colourful Tasmanian names', *Placenames Australia*, March, p. 3.

Flannery, T 1994, *The Future Eaters: An Ecological History of the Australasian Lands and People*, Reed Books, Melbourne.

Gilbert, K 1978, *Living Black: Blacks Talk to Kevin Gilbert*, Penguin, Melbourne, p. 3.

Giles, E 1889, *Australia Twice Traversed: The Romance of Exploration, being a Narrative Compiled from the Journals of Five Exploring Expeditions into and through Central South Australia, and Western Australia, from 1872 to 1876*. <eBooks@Adelaide> 2004, rendered into HTML on 21 June 2002 by Steve Thomas for the University of Adelaide Library Electronic Texts Collection.

Grenville, K 2005, *The Secret River*, Text Publishing, Melbourne, p. 313.

References

Grisham, J 2003, *The King of Torts*, Dell Books, New York.

Harmstorf, I & Cigler, M 1985, *The Germans in Australia*, Australia Ethnic Press, Melbourne.

Hercus, L, Hodges, F & Simpson, J 2002, *The Land is a Map: Placenames of Indigenous Origin in Australia*, Pandanus Books, Canberra.

Hungerford, M E & Donald, J K 1982, *Exploring the Blue Mountains*, Kangaroo Press, Kenthurst, pp. 187–88.

Kaluski, M 1983, *The Poles in Australia*, Australian Ethnic Press, Melbourne, pp. 137–41.

Kennedy, B & B 1989, *Australian Place Names*, Hodder & Stoughton, Melbourne.

Kostanski, L 2003, 'Researching placenames of the Murray River, *Placenames Australia*, December, pp. 4–5.

Lacey, S & M 2003, 'Brand issues', *Sydney Morning Herald*, June 14–15.

Lambert, J 2004, 'Just for fun', *Placenames Australia,* June, p. 11.

Liebecke, T 2004, 'ANPS research friend', Australian Placenames, June, p. 11.

Loots, H 1998, 'Between Jerusalem and Acropolis', newsletter of the Harbourside Group of the Australian Plants Society, June, <http://farrer. riv.csu.edu.au/ASGAP/APOL17/ac00-01.html>.

Low, J 1994, *Pictorial Memories Blue Mountains*, Atrand, Crows Nest.

McKenna, M 2002, *Looking for Blackfellas' Point: An Australian History of Place,* University of NSW Press, Sydney, p. 45.

Manly Daily 1996, ninetieth anniversary souvenir edition.

Manly–Warringah Journal of Local History 1992, vol 5, no 1, November.

Monteath, P 2003, 'Exploring Terra Australia', *History Today*, January, pp. 48–55.

Mulholland, W E 1983, *The Town that Saved Queensland*, National Trust of Queensland, Brisbane.

Noble, B 2004, 'Yanyuwa placenames', *Placenames Australia*, June, pp. 6–7.

Ochert, M 2002, 'Jewish place names', *Australian Jewish Historical Society,* no 58, November–December.

Ollif, L 1975 *There Must be a River: history of the Hornsby Shire*, Ollif Publishing Co, Sydney.

Pascoe, B 2003, 'Aboriginal placenames of Corangamite', *Placenames Australia,* December, pp. 10–11.

Pepworth, B 1981, *Historic Places of Australia*, Macmillan, Melbourne.

Petrick, J 1996, *The History of Alice Springs Through Landmarks and Street Names*, Alice Springs.

Placenames Australia 2005, 'Placenames in the news', March, p. 2.

Pollon, F 1988, *The Book of Sydney Suburbs*, Harper Collins, Sydney.

Readers Digest Illustrated Guide to Australian Places 2003, Readers Digest, Sydney, pp. 366, 487.

Reed, A W 1973, *Place Names of Australia*, A H & A W Reed, Sydney.

Reynolds, G 1992, *German Place Names in Australia Changed During the Great War*, Possum Printing, Batemans Bay.

Richards, C 2002, 'French placenames on the Victorian coast', *Placenames Australia*, March, pp. 2–3.

Richards, C 2004, *Cornish Placenames in Victoria: An Overview*, Cornish Association of Victoria, Melbourne.

Scone and Upper Hunter Historical Society Newsletter 1972, August, p. 7.

Simpson, J 2001, 'Hypocoristics of place-names in Australian English', in Blair, D, Collins, P & Benjamins J (eds.), *English in Australia*, John Benjamins, Amsterdam.

Simpson, J 12 April 2003, 'Naming the land', *Lingua Franca*, ABC Radio National, <http://www.abc.net.au/rn/arts/ling/stories/s830412.htm>.

Stanton, I 1995, *Bridging the Gap: The History of Hall's Gap from 1840*, Victoria.

Stilgoe, R 2004, 'The naming of Como', *Placenames Australia*, March, p. 11.

Stokes, J L 1846 *Discoveries in Australia: Voyages of HMS Beagle* (two volumes), T & W Boone, London.

Taylor, R 2002, 'Lubra Creek', in Bonyhady, T & Griffiths, T (eds.), *Words for Country: Landscape and Language in Australia*, University of NSW Press, Sydney.

Thogersen, J 2001, '*Sydney Harbour Place Names*', <http://www.boatingoz.com.au/articles/sydharnames.htm>.

Trent, J 2003, 'ANPS research friend', *Placenames Australia*, December, p. 9.

Turvey, B 2001, 'Placename in focus — Crows Nest, Queensland', *Placenames Australia*, December, p. 3.

Warton, G 2005, 'Pennefather River, an ever-changing placename', *Placenames Australia*, September, pp. 1–5.

Whittaker, M & Willesee, A 2002, *The Road to Mount Buggery: A Journey Through the Curiously Named Places of Australia*, Pan Macmillan, Sydney, pp. 29, 109, 204–07.

Webography

The following websites were consulted and active during the research for this book.

<http://au/geocities.com>
<http://en.wikipedia.org/wiki/Sydney%2C_Australia#History>
<http://etext.library.adelaide.edu.au/g/giles/ernest/g47a/part34.html>
<http://farrer.riv.csu.edu.au/ASGAP/APOL17/ac00-01.html>
<http://walkabout.com.au/AtoZ/index.shtml>
<http://walkabout.com.au/locations/TASHobart.shtml#Things%20to%20see>
<http://walkabout.com.au/locations/WAPerth.shtml>
<http://www.ahc.sa.gov.au/site/page.cfm?u=208>
<http://www.albury-wodonga.com/docs/history.htm>
<http://www.arts.monash.edu.au/ncas/multimedia/gazetteer>

References

<http://www.arts.usyd.edu.au/departs/linguistics/research/hypocoristic>
<http://www.australiaonthemap.org.au/about.html>
<http://www.bmcc.nsw.gov.au/index.cfm?L1=1&L2=28&L3=31&L4=197&Item=21>
<http://www.boatingoz.com.au/articles/sydharnames.htm>
<http://www.brettdavis.com.au/book/anne.html>
<http://www.cultureandrecreation.gov.au/articles/explorers>
<http://www.gnb.nsw.gov.au>
<http://www.hawkesbury.nsw.gov.au/community/1013/1044.html>
<http://www.icsm.gov.au/icsm/cgna/aboriginal_names.pdf>
<http://www.lpe.nt.gov.au/heritage/register/channel/default.htm>
<http://www.lpe.nt.gov.au/place/maindb.htm>
<http://www.lpe.nt.gov.au/place/ntplaces/greaterdwn.htm>
<http://www.maroochylibraries.qld.gov.au/placenames.htm>
<http://www.ncc.nsw.gov.au/services/culture/library/research/localstudies/place.cfm>
<http://www.newcastle.nsw.gov.au/services/culture/library/research/localstudies/place.cfm>
<http://www.nnsw.com.au/npa/nationalpark.html>
<http://www.ourindooroopilly.com/brisbane-river-map.html>
<http://www.penrithcity.nsw.gov.au>
<http://www.teachers.ash.org.au/dnutting/germanaustralia/e/ortsnamensa.htm>
<http://www.tourisminternet.com.au/chdoma10.htm>
<http://www.tourismtasmania.com.au/media/pr/1999/pr990628.html>
<http://www.travelmate.com.au/Places>
<http://www.ucaqld.com.au/~piula/Placenames/page1.htm>
<http://www.willoughby.nsw.gov.au/_Upload/files/Fact_Castlecrag.pdf>
<http://www.wwt.com.au/townstuv.htm>
<www.arts.monash.edu.au/ncas/multimedia/gazetteer/hist/waverley.html>
<www.dola.wa.gov.au/corporate.nsf/web/History+of+suburb+names>
<www.gnb.nsw.gov.au>
<www.lpe.nt.gov.au/place/maindb.htm>
<www.walkabout.com.au>